MEDIA in GCSE English

Chris Purple
Principal Examiner for EDEXCEL GCSE English

John O'Connor

OXFORD

OXFORD

UNIVERSITY PRESS

Great Clarendon Street, Oxford OX2 6DP

Oxford University Press is a department of the University of Oxford.
It furthers the University's objective of excellence in research, scholarship,
and education by publishing worldwide in

Oxford New York

Auckland Bangkok Buenos Aires Cape Town
Chenai Dar es Salaam Delhi Hong Kong Istanbul Karachi
Kolkata Kuala Lumpur Madrid Melbourne Mexico City Mumbai Nairobi
São Paulo Shanghai Taipei Tokio Toronto

Oxford is a registered trade mark of Oxford University Press
in the UK and in certain other countries

First published 1999
10,9,8,7

Printed in Spain

ISBN 0 19 831454 X

Contents

SECTION 2   Tackling the media paper

SECTION 3   Sample questions

Introduction

If you are taking an English GCSE exam, you will be asked to analyse and comment on media texts. This book has been written to help you do so.

But knowing about media texts – how they're put together, and the impact they can have on you – won't just be useful in examinations. Media texts are all around you, and it's important to be able to judge them for yourself. You need to understand how some media texts try to manipulate you into thinking and acting in particular ways.

Have you ever bought a product because you were taken in by a slick piece of advertising, rather than because you decided it was something you needed or wanted? Or have you formed an opinion based on a newspaper story, only to discover later that the story was inaccurate or misleading?

Media in GCSE English aims to show how media texts are constructed to influence how we think and react.

In **Section 1** we look at aspects of newspaper reports, advertisements, brochures and leaflets. We help you to understand how language is used in special ways in media texts and give you practice in analysing and writing about these techniques. There are ten units on Newspapers and ten on Advertising.

The first three units on Newspapers aim to establish the facts about newspapers which you need to know: the characteristics of tabloids and broadsheets; the range of articles to be encountered; the part played by design. The remaining seven units focus on features of newspaper *language*.

Similarly, the first four units on Advertising take a general look at the subject: who advertises, the different sorts of printed advertising material they use, the groups they are targeting, and how design increases the impact of advertising. The remaining six units then explore the language of advertising.

Section 2 looks more closely at examination technique – how to use your time effectively, and how to analyse questions so that you produce relevant, focused answers. Exam technique matters because you have limited time to demonstrate your reading and writing skills and the examiner won't give you credit for doing things which are not relevant to the questions on the paper. We look in detail at some actual examination answers and show you what candidates did well and how they could have improved their answers. The general advice in this section is also relevant to other English examinations, as well as those in other subjects where you need to produce developed written responses.

Section 3 gives you the opportunity to practise for the examination. It contains five complete two-hour examination papers, each consisting of one reading question and two writing questions. These papers follow the structure of the Edexcel Media paper but the questions are similar to those which you can expect to be set by any of the other GCSE boards.

Although the texts we look at in this book are all drawn from print-based media, many of the ideas behind them can be applied more widely – to television, cinema, radio, E-mail and the Internet. For example, if you understand the persuasive techniques which are being used in a printed advertisement, you should also be able to recognize similar techniques in a television advertisement. And if you understand how a newspaper report is organized and written, you will also be able to apply your understanding to television or radio news reports. So if you are following a GCSE Media Studies course, you will find this book helpful, too.

Don't restrict your thinking about media texts to lessons and homework assignments. When you're reading a football report, a fashion story or a story about a celebrity, think about how it's written and presented. If you're walking past an advertisement on a hoarding, stop and think about how the visual image and the written word work together to persuade you to buy a product or accept an idea.

Above all, think about and react to what you see and read. Be alert to the ways in which writers' choices in language and structure may deliberately create particular impressions, which could be fair or unfair. Be prepared to enjoy the humour and wit of advertisements even though you may have no interest in the products they are trying to sell. But look out too for advertisements which build up misleading impressions yet stop short of telling lies.

We hope that this book helps you to understand and to judge media texts for yourself. We also hope that it helps to give you the knowledge and confidence to answer your examination questions effectively.

Chris Purple
John O'Connor

Broadsheets and tabloids

| Learning aims | ▶ To understand the terms **broadsheet** and **tabloid**. |
| | ▶ To identify the key characteristics of broadsheet and tabloid newspapers. |

Facts

▶ The terms broadsheet and tabloid originally referred purely to the newspaper's size – a broadsheet's pages are twice the size of a tabloid's.

▶ Although there are many more similarities than differences between broadsheet and tabloid newspapers, each type does tend to have certain characteristics.

Broadsheets

▶ The national daily and Sunday broadsheets include the *Times*, the *Financial Times*, the *Independent*, the *Guardian*, the *Daily Telegraph*, the *Sunday Times*, the *Sunday Telegraph*, the *Independent on Sunday* and the *Observer*. These newspapers are sometimes referred to as the 'quality' or 'serious' press.

▶ Broadsheet newspapers are aimed at social groupings A, B and C1.
  ▶ Examples from group A include lawyers, doctors, and accountants.
  ▶ Examples from group B include teachers, nurses, and police officers.
  ▶ Examples from group C1 include clerical workers and people in other skilled jobs.

Tabloids

▶ The national daily and Sunday tabloids include the *Mirror*, the *Sun*, the *Sunday Mirror*, the *People* and the *News of the World*. These are sometimes called the 'popular' tabloids.

▶ Tabloid newspapers are aimed at social groupings C2, D and E.
  ▶ Examples from group C2 include plumbers and mechanics.
  ▶ Examples from group D include lorry drivers and postal workers.
  ▶ Examples from group E include unemployed people and casual workers.

▶ The *Daily Express* and the *Daily Mail* are sometimes referred to as 'middle-range' or 'middle-of-the-road' tabloids, because they aim for an audience which might otherwise read a broadsheet newspaper.

Broadsheet newspapers
Broadsheets tend to have the following features:

Kneeling at the feet of Blair

- More extensive and more detailed political news
- A higher proportion of longer articles

Sainsbury's £5m for Tate

- Wider coverage of cultural news
- 'Upmarket' social flavour, aimed at social groups A, B and C1

1,500 coal jobs at risk

- Industrial news
- A plainer and more restrained layout

INTERNATIONAL NEWS
Africa 'looks to Nigeria'

More extensive attention paid to international news

Barclays joins £2bn market rescue

- A greater focus on financial matters
- More 'serious' articles

Tabloid newspapers
Tabloids tend to be different in a number of ways:

Missed her ... and Mrs

STEFAN WEDS THE GIRL NEXT DOOR HE AVOIDED FOR 15 YRS

Bolder layout

More 'human interest' stories

£950m toll of booze cruise smugglers

'Downmarket' approach aimed at social groups C2, D and E

KIT KAT'S A HANDFUL

A higher proportion of shorter articles, covered in less depth

Read and discuss

In your exam, you may be presented with articles from either a tabloid or a broadsheet newspaper. Therefore, it is important that you know what each term means and how they differ from each other.

Below are two lists of articles, labelled A and B, along with their lengths in numbers of words. These articles appeared in the opening pages of two national newspapers, the *Mirror* and the *Guardian* on 15 October 1998. Alongside each list is another list of handwritten notes describing each article.

1 Discuss which of the handwritten notes matches each article.

2 Now, try to identify lists A and B. Which is the tabloid list and which is the broadsheet? Give reasons for your answer.

NEWSPAPER A

Article

CLINTON FACES NEW ATTACK

(750 words)

FLYING SQUAD OFFICERS ADMIT CRIME CAREER

(750 words)

THIS WAY TO THE SCAFFOLD

(650 words and two colour photographs, 21 x 15 and 6 x 4 cms)

CAMBRIDGE DON'S NOBEL ETHICS

(650 words and a 21 x 20 cm black and white photograph)

77 DEATHS PROBED IN GP MURDER ENQUIRY

(350 words and a 6 x 4 cm black and white photograph)

FRESH INTERPRETATION FROM THE RSC

(550 words)

Description

Theatre review on a Royal Shakespeare Company play

Story about the investigation into the deaths of a doctor's patients

International political report

News story about the move to change the House of Lords

News story about the police and their anti-corruption drive

Report about a Cambridge University professor winning the Nobel Prize

NEWSPAPER B

Article

BIG BROTHER IS WATCHING

(550 words)

BREAKING UP IS SO SAD, SAYS DIAMOND

(120 words and a 14 x 13 cm colour photograph)

MURDER POLICE PROBE FILES OF 150 PATIENTS

(450 words and a 6 x 5 cm black and white photograph)

CAMILLA AND HER DAUGHTER THE BELLES OF THE BOWLES

(almost the whole page, including two colour photographs, each of 29 x 9 cm)

ANDREW'S PR GIRL TIRED OF THE ROYAL ROLE REVERSAL

(300 words)

Description

Story about the investigation into the deaths of a doctor's patients

Follow-up to yesterday's story about the break-up of Prince Andrew's relationship with Aurelia Cecil

Prince Charles's friend, Camilla Parker-Bowles attends a fashionable party with her daughter

Story of Anne Diamond's marriage break-up

Report on a new closed-circuit television system designed to catch criminals

---

Write

1 Under the headings 'tabloid' and 'broadsheet', make two lists of what you consider to be the particular strengths and attractive features of both types of newspaper.

2 Then, using the ideas from one of your lists, create a simple advertisement which begins: 'This is what you get for your money if you buy... '(adding the name of either a tabloid or broadsheet newspaper). Use some of the headlines in this unit as examples of articles or features which will attract readers to your chosen newspaper. You don't need to use pictures or drawings; instead concentrate on choosing the right words.

Homework

1 Choose a broadsheet and a tabloid newspaper published on the same day.

2 Look through the papers and make notes on the different amounts of page space (measured in numbers of words) that they devote to **one** or **two** of the same news stories.

3 Which important news stories (in your opinion) appear more prominently in one paper, or appear in one newspaper but not at all in the other?

4 What do you think are the attitudes of the two newspapers to their readers?

▶ What do they think their readers are interested in?

▶ How do they think their readers like to have their stories presented to them?

Articles

Learning aims	▶ To be aware of the **range** and **variety** of articles in newspapers. ▶ To be clear about the different **purposes** that articles can serve.

Facts	▶ Newspapers clearly contain more than just 'news'; they include different kinds of articles for different purposes. For example, **news reports** are about immediate events while **features** take a broader look at a subject.
	
	▶ Articles will
	  ▶ cover different **topics** (e.g. politics, fashion, television programmes)
	  ▶ be intended for different **audiences** (e.g. a wide audience, women, sports fans)
	  ▶ take different **forms** (e.g. news reports, features, letters)
	  ▶ be written for different **purposes** (e.g. to inform, to persuade, to entertain readers).
	
	▶ The balance of different articles and sections will change from one newspaper to another.

This is a representation of some of the many different articles and features to be found in national newspapers. They all appeared in the *Daily Express* on 21 July, 1998.

LEAD STORY
(front page)

EXCLUSIVE STORY
(pages 14-15)

BLAIR'S ONE NATION PLEDGE

Selected as the most important or dramatic story that day and often continued on the inside pages

EXCLUSIVE: Blair aims to reclaim city streets

THE GOVERNMENT'S PLAN TO BANISH BIG BROTHER

People taught to help themselves

Although papers often claim that a story is 'exclusive' to them, it may well appear elsewhere. This one, featuring the Prime Minister, is a follow-up to the front page story and is considered important and interesting enough to justify a double-page spread

MEDIA STORY
(page 3)

My pathetic BBC boss Birt, by Anna

Taking up almost the whole page, and in a prominent position, this is expected to be of wide interest to readers, as it features BBC celebrities and a controversy

LEADER ARTICLE
(page 10)

THE EXPRESS

Save sink estates from going down the plughole

Here the editorial team puts forward its own opinions about important news items. The leader represents the newspaper's philosophy and political viewpoint

FASHION FEATURE
(page 13)

Dazzling Dior's touch of Tudor

The text of this article is quite brief – most of the page is taken by colour photographs

INSIDE STORY
(page 17)

Pill that will cut asthma attacks

Considered interesting enough to justify an article, but not sufficiently so to be on the front or opening pages

OVERSEAS NEWS
(page 20)

AROUND THE WORLD

Nigeria's pledge for democracy

HUMAN INTEREST STORY
(page 21)

£1.5m for the pilot crippled by jet blast

Usually accompanied by a photograph

CONSUMER REPORT
(page 21)

Stores defy designer labels ban

A spotlight on 'the shopping basket'

LIGHT-HEARTED STORY
(page 23)

Alarming aria stops the show

Dame Kiri opera is halted by ringing handbag

Something designed to amuse or intrigue the reader

LETTERS PAGE
(page 26)

Letters

Please write to: Letters to The Editor, The Express, 245 Blackfriars Road, London SE1 9UX.
FAX: 0171 922 7055/7794; TELEPHONE: 0171 928 7311.
e-mail: express.letters@express.co.uk
Letters must include address and telephone number.

Letter of the Day

At least let us eat in peace

Some newspapers have a mixture of serious and light-hearted correspondence

TELEVISION REVIEW
(page 41)

LAST NIGHT'S TELEVISION

Nothing too Fawlty about the new hotel sitcom. **By Nigel Billen**

HOROSCOPE
(page 46)

STARS

By Marjorie Orr *Britain's top astrologer*

BUSINESS AND FINANCE
(page 47)

Bus firms in tussle

EXTENDED SPORTS REPORT
(page 56)

Testing time for Atherton

A full and detailed report

BRIEF SPORTS REPORT
(page 60)

Nicola strikes gold again
SWIMMING

This gives the main details only

Read and discuss   It is important to be able to recognize an article by its 'type', such as a leader, a feature or a news report.

1 The cuttings below are all headlines of articles; read them carefully.

2 Then, using the examples on pages 13–15 from the *Daily Express* as a guide, decide what kind of article each one is.

£6bn ROADS PLAN AXED

OWEN FEELS HEAT

Fashion   FEMAIL

Facing up to winter

DAILY MAIL COMMENT

Making the Lords leap in the dark
lead story.

Hunt protesters pledge to fight on

Pride tinged with sorrow for Paul the solo parent

Van Dyck is offered to Tate – and the taxman

Blood tonic for donors
inside story

Play fair over the euro, Hague warns Labour

Hell's Angel Fish
It may look pretty, but it could zap you with its death ray

Write

If you are presented with a newspaper article in the exam, it is important to ask yourself the following questions:
- ▶ What is the topic of this article?
- ▶ What kind of audience is it aimed at?
- ▶ What form is it in - feature, leader, news report, etc.?
- ▶ What is its purpose?

1 Copy and fill in the table below with as many examples as you can from the cuttings in this unit. Three have already been added to start you off.

ARTICLE	TOPIC	AUDIENCE	FORM	PURPOSE
Blair's One Nation Pledge	politics	general	news report	to inform (and persuade)
Dazzling Dior's Touch of Tudor	fashion	people interested in fashion	feature	to entertain and inform
Alarming Aria Stops the Show	opera	general	news report	to entertain

2 Then with a partner, compare your grids and discuss any differences in your findings. Remember, there will not always be a 'correct' answer.

3 Look carefully at the column headed 'Purpose'. How many differences can you find here? Are there more differences here than in the other columns?

Homework

Find a recent copy of a national newspaper of your choice and fill in a grid like the one above which will show as wide a variety of articles as possible. Try to include articles that are very different in their 'purpose'.

The Daily Telegraph

[1]

★ ★ No. 44,484

45p

[2] Thursday, June 25, 1998

[3] Britain's biggest-selling quality daily

Plus

appointments

Now with Fax Back
Our new service for readers

[4] We name
the Pothole of
the Year

The Daily Telegraph Campaign
for Better Roads, Page 17

[4] My brother,
Frank Sinatra,
by Tony Bennett

Interview by Michael Shelden
Features, Page 26

connected
Thursday's 16-page section

---

[5] Bombers target Ulster vote

[6] Village is torn apart by blast on eve of poll

[8] By Toby Harnden
In Newtownhamilton

THE centre of a Northern Ireland village was blown apart yesterday by a republican car bomb detonated on the eve of Ulster's [7] _____ bly elections.

A teenage boy w____red and the local polling station was badly damaged in what both Unionist and nationalist politicians condemned as an attack on democracy.

Two warnings of the attack were telephoned, one purporting to be from the Irish National Liberation Army splinter group, giving less than an hour for the village of Newtownhamilton, Co Armagh, to be cleared by the Royal Ulster Constabulary.

The condition of a 15-year-old boy hit in the chest by debris was described last night as "stable". Several people were treated for shock.

A number of buildings in the predominantly Roman Catholic village may have to be demolished. Among those worst damaged was the community centre, which was due to be used as a polling station. There was little damage to the security base.

Garnet Mullan, principal of Newtownhamilton High

Picture: MAX NASH/AP

[10]

Blair softens euro stance after Sun offensive

By George Jones, Political Editor

TONY Blair yesterday toned down his enthusiasm for the European single currency after a fierce counterblast from Rupert Murdoch's *Sun* newspaper.

The paper, which supported Labour at the election, branded the Prime Minister potentially "the most dangerous man in Britain" because of signs that the Government favoured early entry to monetary union.

Although Mr Blair told the Commons he would not change his policy as a result of the newspaper's campaign, he injected a new sense of coolness into the Government's rhetoric.

He said the Government was refusing to rule out joining a single currency "as a matter of principle", and stressed the economic tests that would have to be satisfied before it would consider giving up the pound.

This was a significant change of emphasis from last week's European summit in Cardiff, at which Mr Blair appeared to be adopting the role of "persuader" on a single currency. He described it then as a "turning point" for Europe and suggested it could herald a long period of mon currency that I don't

age" confirmed that the media was obsessed with itself.

"The *Sun* has a well-known position on the single currency and the fact that it restates it doesn't strike me as terribly newsworthy," said Mr Campbell.

"I just wonder: is it the second most important thing happening in the world today?" he asked. "I cannot think it is."

The *Sun*'s front page was dominated by a photograph of Mr Blair and the headline: "Is THIS the most dangerous man in Britain?"

Inside, it carried a further picture of Mr Blair in a mask. It said that while Mr Blair was a fine Prime Minister in most respects, "he seems determined to scrap 'the pound and take Britain into the single currency".

David Yelland, the recently-appointed editor of the *Sun*, insisted the paper had been forced to ask its readers to "think the unthinkable" because of Mr Blair's persuasive talents.

"It is because of his ability to persuade people that he could be the most dangerous man in Britain, because he could be taking us into a com-

[9]

sign of that in Newtownhamilton today."

Yesterday's explosion was the latest in a series of republican bomb attacks originating from the South Armagh border area since Sinn Fein joined the Northern Ireland talks in September. Parties in favour of the agreement feared its timing might undermine support for David a bomb blast in nearby Drumintee intended to kill members of a joint Army and RUC patrol. Security sources have said continued terrorist activity in the area could force the shelving of plans to dismantle security installations.

More than a million people are expected to vote today in the first opportunity to shape a devolved administration voter apathy could undermine the Stormont agreement signed on Good Friday.

The Newtownhamilton attack appeared to strengthen the hand of Ian Paisley, the Democratic Unionist Party leader, and other hardline Unionists opposed to the agreement.

"This [South Armagh] is Provo country and nothing British Government to buckle under republican pressure."

One senior security source, however, said it was highly unlikely that the attack was sanctioned or approved of by the IRA leadership. "IRA members might have been involved but this attack is as likely designed to undermine Gerry Adams and Sinn Fein months in Enniskillen, Moira and Portadown are thought to have been the work of IRA dissidents.

Ken Maginnis, the Ulster Unionist Party security spokesman, said Sinn Fein should establish its democratic credentials by condemning the attack.

He added: "Those who are suggesting there may be a

Paul Murphy, Northern Ireland's political development minister, urged voters not to be intimidated by the Newtownhamilton bomb. "This act of violence is against the spirit of all that the people of Northern Ireland have embraced for the future," he said.

Attack on democracy: Page 2

But there was nervousness that the *Sun*, Mr Blair's most powerful supporter in the media, might be adopting a more critical stance.

Alastair Campbell, the Prime Minister's press secretary, criticised the BBC for giving the newspaper's report prominent coverage on yesterday's morning news.

He said the "excited cover-

The *Sun*'s attack was greeted with delight by the Conservatives and coincided with a speech by Francis Maude, the shadow Chancellor, setting out the economic case on which they oppose

Continued on Page 2

Maude onslaught: Page 6
Alice Thomson: Page 30
Editorial Comment: Page 31

16

'At first it's all right and then suddenly the ball appears in the back of our goal'

12

on the **Internet:**
electronic
http://www.tele .uk

14

The Daily Telegraph 25-6-98

9 770307 123641 26

15

A B C D E F

The Prue Leith recipe for cool lord lieutenant

11

By Philip Johnston, Home Affairs Editor

TONY BLAIR'S campaign to modernise Britain's institutions has been extended to the ancient office of lord lieutenant, with the cookery expert Prue Leith appearing on a list of candidates for the forthcoming London vacancy.

The post has traditionally been filled by a senior Army officer and is currently held by Field Marshall Lord Bramall, a former chief of the defence staff.

The favourite to succeed him on his retirement this year was a fellow officer, Field Marshall Sir John Chapple, a deputy lieutenant of London and former Governor and Commander in Chief of Gibraltar.

However, Downing Street is anxious to broaden the selection base to include more women and more candidates from the ethnic minority communities. It has submitted a shortlist to Buckingham Palace and, although the final choice is theoretically within the Queen's gift, it is understood that Miss Leith is the Government's preferred choice.

An Asian businesswoman and Sir Colin Marshall, chairman of British Airways, are also said to be under consideration.

There are around 100 lord lieutenants acting as the representatives of the Crown in each county of the United Kingdom. They are appointed by the Queen on the advice of the Prime Minister and may be peers or commoners.

The post was created in 1557 under Henry VIII with the original task of taking over the military duties of the Sheriff and controlling the military forces of the Crown.

Leith: celebrity cook

Today, their duties include responsibility for royal visits to their county, chairing the body that appoints magistrates and handing out awards such as the Queen's Scout and Guide badges.

Present incumbents hail from some of the country's great aristocratic and commercial families. They include Samuel Whitbread, of the brewing dynasty; Sir Timothy Colman, of the mustard family; the Duke of Buccleuch and Queensberry, and Viscount Ridley of Northumberland.

A Downing Street spokesman said that candidates were being considered for

Continued on Page 2

Editorial Comment: Page 31

17

Rusedski is out of Wimbledon

11

By Susie Steiner

GREG Rusedski, the British fourth seed, pulled out of Wimbledon yesterday because of an ankle injury, intensifying the pressure on his compatriot, Tim Henman.

The Canadian-born player, who announced his decision moments before he was due to play on Court No 1, also said that he had split with his coach, Tony Pickard.

"Tony feels he doesn't want to work with me anymore and that's it," said Rusedski. "So the relationship is basically over."

Pickard had advised Rusedski not to risk long-term injury by playing but Rusedski had ignored him and went on court on Tuesday.

"There's no longer the trust between us," said Pickard. "Over the last two weeks, there was a total breakdown in communication."

Rusedski responded to his former coach's remarks by saying: "If that's the way he feels, fine. I think the timing of it is a little suspect."

Henman, speaking after beating David Nainkin yesterday, said: "The expectation and attention that we have for these couple of weeks is pretty intense. I am quite happy just to concentrate on what I'm doing."

Reports: Pages 44 and 48

6-goal Spain out

Spain went out of the World Cup last night, despite beating Bulgaria 6-1, after Paraguay beat Nigeria 3-1. France beat Denmark 2-1 — both qualify — and South Africa and Saudi Arabia drew 2-2.

Reports: Pages 3, 42, 43 & 48

BBC could lose Test matches in TV shake-up

By Robert Shrimsley, Chief Political Correspondent

TEST match cricket is to lose the protected status which guarantees that games in England are shown on terrestrial television following a review of sporting events. Chris Smith, the Culture Secretary, will announce today.

The move is likely to see the loss of most BBC live television coverage of the domestic Test match season.

Mr Smith will tell MPs that he no longer sees any justification for preventing satellite television from buying exclusive rights to show Test cricket.

He will argue that the list of protected events exists to secure events with great national resonance like the FA Cup final, Wimbledon and the Grand National and that there is no longer any reason to see Test matches in that light.

Westminster sources said last night that, although the main outcome of the review was a change in Test match status, it would also lead to the creation of a new B list of events whose highlights must be made available to terrestrial television.

The cricket World Cup, due to be held in England next year, will be on the B list, guaranteeing highlights for terrestrial television.

The news will delight cricket bosses who have lobbied hard for the right to sell their coverage to the highest bidder, even if it means the live television coverage is available only on satellite or cable. They believe it will bring substantial new revenue into the game which they can plough back into improving resources and helping to nurse a new generation of top talent.

The English Cricket Board is expected to ensure that at least one Test — probably the Lord's match — is preserved for coverage by the BBC in order to maintain large audiences for the sport.

One senior source stressed that the decision would not affect BBC radio coverage on Test Match Special.

The decision has looked likely ever since an advisory committee, which included Jack Charlton and Steve Cram, recommended a complete overhaul of the list.

Mr Smith is expected to reject a recommendation that he cut back the protected status of the football World Cup to the final stage matches and games involving home teams. The entire tournament will remain protected.

The committee's original recommendation to Mr Smith was that the A list should be: the Olympic Games; the World Cup finals (final, semi-finals and matches involving home nations); the European Football Championships (final, semi-finals and matches involving home teams); the FA Cup final; the Scottish FA Cup final; Wimbledon (the finals weekend); the Grand National; and the Derby.

BBC sport chief quits: Page 3

17

Design

Learning aims	▶ To understand how **design features** are used in order to attract readers and to present articles in interesting ways.
Facts	▶ There is fierce competition to sell newspapers. To attract busy commuters, the front page has to be clearly set out, instantly recognizable as belonging to that particular newspaper and striking enough to catch the eye. ▶ That is why, while there are significant differences between national tabloids and local newspapers in content, they have many design features in common. ▶ Design is used both to attract readers and to present material in interesting, effective and eye-catching ways.

Look at the example of the front page from the *Daily Telegraph* on pages 18-19. The numbers (on the front page and the corresponding notes below) refer to typical features of newspaper design and layout.

1 Masthead
traditional 'gothic' lettering

2 Publishing information

3 Slogan
advertises the newspaper itself

4 'Puffs' or 'Blurbs'
colour band aims to attract readers to inside features or stories

5 Headlines
largest size for the most important stories

6 Sub-heads
expand upon the headline

7 Lead story
something of interest to the whole nation

8 By-line
details of the journalist who has written the article

9 Secondary lead
important, but less dramatic than the main story

10 Colour photographs
to add a visual dimension

11 Different type sizes
for clarity and variety

12 Menu
picks out the sections frequently consulted by readers

13 Display ad
large enough for text and photo

14 Small ad

15 Bar code

16 Cartoon
based upon a current news story

17 Links with other articles inside

Read and discuss

In your exam, you may be asked to comment on what contribution the design features make to the overall impact of a newspaper article. Look carefully at the front page of the *Daily Telegraph* on pages 18-19 and try to answer the following questions.

1 How effective is the main photograph as an eye-catcher? Do you think that it encourages people to buy the newspaper? If so, why?

2 What does the main photograph add to the written report? You might want to think about the following things:
  ▶ the composition of the photograph - who or what is in it and where they are placed - including the relationship of the soldier to the buildings
  ▶ the fact that the photograph is taken from the soldier's viewpoint
  ▶ the colour.

3 Why does this newspaper use coloured print and photographs on the front page?
  Here are some things to think about:
  ▶ the blue band near the top of the page
  ▶ the effect of the three other splashes of colour in leading the eye to the lower half of the page.
  Do they work?

4 What effect does the newspaper hope to create by:
  ▶ the variety of headline sizes
  ▶ the use of different fonts (type styles).
  Is it successful?

Write

1 Think of a gripping news item and, using the Newtownhamilton bombing article as a model, draw a rough sketch of how it might be designed for the front page of the *Daily Telegraph*, to include a written report and a photograph.

2 Make up an eye-catching headline, sub-head and by-line for your story. Then write the first few lines of the report including a caption to the photograph.

3 Then add notes and arrows to highlight and explain the features that you have included in your sketch.

4 Finally, you could sketch out a draft plan for the whole front page.

Homework

1 Take the front page from an edition of any national or local newspaper and paste it on to a larger sheet of paper to create a margin on all sides.

2 Then using the example from the *Daily Telegraph* on pages 18-19 as a model, make notes in the margin and use arrows to show the design features used on your front page.

3 Add further notes to comment on any differences that you notice between the example from the *Daily Telegraph* and your chosen front page.

Headlines and journalese

Learning aims	▶ To understand the uses and effectiveness of **wordplay** in headline writing. ▶ To become familiar with **journalese shorthand** and the way it is used in headlines.
Facts	▶ Newspapers employ many methods to make their headlines eye-catching, dramatic and memorable. ▶ A common headline technique is to use a play on words based on the subject of the story. ▶ To save space and attract the reader's attention, headline writers have developed their own vocabulary of short, dramatic words.

Wordplay

These word-playing headlines all appeared within a few weeks of each other.

Puns on names

These are especially popular with football journalists.

CHRISTIAN PRAYS FOR SALVATION
Tottenham put a stop to Gross incompetence

Spurs are losing matches under their manager, Christian Gross, who finally leaves the club

ANGEL'S WINGING HIS WAY TO WBA

Oxford United winger Mark Angel is to join West Bromwich Albion

THIEVES SHOW SHEAR-ER CHEEK

A cardboard Alan Shearer is stolen from outside a shop

Other puns and wordplay

CAT FLAP IN DOWNING STREET

Humphrey, the Number 10 cat, goes missing

BIGGEST OF THE MALL

Manchester's Trafford Park shopping complex opens

WE'VE A WEEVER INVASION ON COAST

An increase of poisonous weever fish on our beaches

SNAKES ALIVE - WE'VE ADDER POPULATION RISE

Number of adders increases rapidly in the summer heat

AD'LL DO NICELY FOR QUEEN MUM

Queen Mother advertises for housemaids

Play on proverbial expressions

TILL DEAF US DO PART

Man deliberately shouts in his wife's ear and damages her hearing

LOVE AT FIRST FLIGHT

RAF romance

Use of colloquial expressions

PLASTIC OWL MAKES A TWIT OF THE LAW
Harassment law gets bird in police swoop

Man arrested for putting a plastic owl in his garden to frighten off his neighbour's pigeons

IT WON'T WASH

Husband's excuse rejected after he had beaten his wife for not putting the washing away

Rhyme **YELL LEFT ME IN HELL**

Woman's ear damaged when her husband deliberately shouts in it

Read and discuss

1 Using examples from the wordplay headlines on page 22 and above, discuss the reasons why journalists
  ▶ create puns on people's names or on the situation reported in the story
  ▶ make humorous use of proverbial or colloquial expressions. What effects are they trying to achieve?

2 Is it appropriate to use jokes and wordplay in headlines concerning serious subjects such as 'wife-abuse'? (See 'Till Deaf...' 'Yell Left Me...' and 'It Won't Wash'.)

Journalese shorthand

Headlines can take up a great deal of space and so journalists have developed their own shorthand vocabulary to produce dramatic, punchy headlines. Some of this vocabulary is rarely used anywhere else and can involve unusual use of nouns, verbs and adjectives.

NOUNS

Police face racism probe

Murdoch in new bid

By-pass fury

Smoking ban in council offices

Tot stops the traffic

Quest for AIDS cure

Police in drugs swoop

New beef scare

Army in mercy dash

VERBS

Rover to axe develoment plan

Tories split on Europe

Johnson quits BBC

Russia hit by recession

Unemployment to top 3 million

Prescott slams motorists

French franc plunges

Blair vows to cut taxes

Temperatures set to rise

Ashdown and Haig clash

Schools to curb smoking

ADJECTIVES

Willets given key post

Army in mercy dash

Read and discuss

1 Look back at the examples of journalese shorthand on page 24 and discuss the following questions:

▶ Which longer word or phrase was replaced by each of the highlighted examples?
▶ Why do you think each of these replacement words has been chosen instead?

2 This headline appeared in the *Guardian* on 24 September 1998: 'Seven Held in Terror Swoop'. Discuss the four examples of journalese shorthand used here.

▶ Which longer words or phrases does each example replace?
▶ Why have they been chosen for this story?

Write

In the exam, it will help if you can spot the wordplay used in a headline. But that on its own is not enough you also need to show that you understand why a particular journalist has chosen to use it and what it adds to the news story.

The headlines below all relate to a particular sports event. Chelsea's manager, Ruud Gullit, was angry that the football match with the Norwegian team, Tromso, had taken place in a blizzard. Gianluca Vialli was the Chelsea goal-scorer.

SNOW JOKE FOR CHILLY CHELSEA

CHILL-SEA

IT'S SNOW JOKE RUUD

RUUD RAGE

VIALLI WARMS THE HEART AS CHELSEA SKATE ON THIN ICE

Iceman Luca Digs Ruudy Out of the Deep Freeze

ARCTIC ROLE: GULLIT PLAYS IT COOL IN TROMSO

Chill-sea are caught cold but Vialli's n-ice pair saves 'em

CHELSEA SURVIVE IN WINTER BLUNDERLAND

1 Write a brief explanation of the wordplay used in each of these headlines.
2 Then, select two or three favourites and explain why they are particularly effective.

| **Homework** | Find further examples of striking headlines. Explain the wordplay in each case and discuss why it works well for that particular news story. |

The structure of newspaper articles

Learning aims	▶ To understand the particular ways in which journalists **organize** their material and **structure** articles.
Facts	▶ Journalists have to write to deadlines and convey sometimes complex issues in short, readable articles.
	▶ Newspaper articles are structured to gain the reader's attention and then keep it as long as possible.
	▶ Journalists writing news reports often introduce the article with the most dramatic and most important fact – the **intro** – and then follow it up with the second most dramatic, then the third, and so on. This is known as **pyramid writing**, because while 100 % of readers might read the headline, only 70% may read to the end of the first paragraph and only 50% to the end of the third (as though in an inverted pyramid). Journalists often say that the intro is the hardest part of the article to write.

The following extract, the opening of an article from the *Daily Mail*, is typical of pyramid writing.

Bangers and rockets are banned in new Bonfire safety drive

Daily Mail Reporter

BANGERS and small rockets have been banned in an attempt to cut the number of deaths and injuries from fireworks this year.

The move extends a crackdown which outlawed the most powerful rockets last year and increased the minimum age for buying fireworks from 16 to 18.

Consumer affairs Minister Dr Kim Howells said the changes in the law were already making Bonfire Night safer.

'Last year there were 908 injuries caused by fireworks, a 26 per cent drop on the previous year – the best decrease for over 23 years,' he added.

'Every firework has the potential to cause injury if handled stupidly, carelessly or

1 The first sentence contains the important, attention-catching fact – the intro

2 The second includes some context – or background information

3 Quotations tend to come lower down the order

27

Below and opposite are jumbled extracts from three news articles. Each extract consists of a headline, an intro and three follow-up sentences.

1 Rearrange each group of muddled sentences into what you believe to be the most effective order.

2 How did you choose which sentences went where?

(3) Mireille Pull and Jean Gautier believed they would never see each other again after their release from the French prison camp while still schoolchildren.

(2) A SISTER and brother who survived six years side-by-side in a Nazi concentration camp before being separated have been reunited after more than 50 years.

(4) She was cared for by nuns as an 11-year old and sent to England to start a new life with a foster family.

(5) He was nine years old and stayed in their native France where they had been imprisoned by Hitler's invading forces.

(1)
Brother and sister are reunited after 50-year separation

By Paul Stokes

(2) AN ATTEMPT to cross the Atlantic by a lone yachtsman in a boat scarcely bigger than a kitchen sink has been abandoned only two days into the voyage after a confrontation with Moroccan fishermen.

(3) Tom McNally's craft *Vera Hugh II*, the smallest to make the attempt, was damaged when it became entangled in their nets off north Africa.

HOME NEWS 5

(1)
Irate fishermen sink sailor's small dream

BY MICHAEL HORSNELL

(5) The former fine arts lecturer from Liverpool, who spent two years building the 3ft 11in vessel, said: 'The water was freezing and I had to keep bobbing under to reach the nets.

(4) Mr McNally, 55, bound for New York from Gibraltar, spent nearly 12 hours cutting through steel cables with a hacksaw only to be confronted by the fishermen who demanded compensation.

SORRY SEEMS TO BE THE HARDEST WORD

Elton fans furious at no apology for cancelled concert

By MATT CHILDE

Billy Joel apologized to fans in a leaflet handed out at the gate — but the statement made no mention of Elton.

But when they arrived at the venue they found the concert has been cancelled after singer-songwriter Joel suffered an asthma attack.

Nurses Jeni Brownlee, 37, Pat Brown, 40, Mary Murray, 30, and Simon Darwin, 30, each paid £35 for tickets to see Elton perform with Billy Joel at the Old Trafford cricket ground, in Manchester, last week.

A GROUP of hard-up Oxford nurses have lashed out at millionaire pop star Sir Elton John for pulling out of a concert they travelled 150 miles to see.

Write

1 In July 1998, a British boat took part in a record-breaking voyage. Imagine that you are the journalist who took the following notes on this story.

The boat was called 'Cable and Wireless Adventurer'

The leader of the all-British crew was Jock Wishart, 46, from Dumfries

It became the fastest powered vessel to circumnavigate the globe

The circumnavigation took 74 days 20 hours and 58 minutes

The boat originally set out from Gibraltar

It was 115 feet long

The whole journey was 26,000 miles

The final leg was across the Atlantic, from New York to Gibraltar

The boat raced to outrun a storm on the final leg and engineers on board had to work hard to fix a leak

2 Write the headline, intro and the second and third paragraphs for the report published in a broadsheet newspaper the following day. Make sure that you use all the facts included in the notes.

Homework

1 Look through a selection of newspapers to find further examples of pyramid writing.

2 Now you are familiar with this technique, use it to write your own report on an item of local or national news which interests you.

Paragraphs

Learning aims	▶ To understand how **paragraphs** are used to structure a newspaper article.
Facts	▶ On the whole, journalists take the view that, in order to keep the reader's attention, paragraphs have to be kept short and snappy. ▶ Therefore, the rules for paragraphing, especially in tabloid newspaper articles, can be different from those followed in other kinds of writing.

Broadsheets generally follow the usual rules for paragraphing: they start a new paragraph for every development in the report or argument. Tabloid newspapers seem to follow their own rules, and their journalists often use very short paragraphs indeed. This article appeared in the *Daily Mail* on 27 November, 1997.

LESSON BAN ON GIRL WHO MADE HERSELF LOOK REALLY SCARY

Nerissa with the stud that led to trouble

A SCHOOLGIRL has been banned from classes after having her tongue pierced like one of the Spice Girls.

Nerissa Sulley, 14, wanted to be the first of her friends to copy their idol Mel B — Scary Spice.

She went with her mother Tracy to a tattoo parlour and paid £30 for a metal bar and stud through her tongue.

Teachers at Montsaye School in Rothwell, Northamptonshire, spotted the silver glittering in her mouth and reported her to headteacher Lawrie Dale.

He told Nerissa it broke strict school rules on jewellery and has said she will be taught on her own unless she takes it out.

He said: 'Nerissa will be taught in a separate, empty classroom. Her class teacher will give her instructions at the start of the lesson and check she has done the work at the end of it. No additional teaching staff will be needed.'

Yesterday Nerissa's 36-year-old mother attacked the decision.

'What's it got to do with them?' she said. 'She doesn't go around sticking her tongue out.

'She works very hard at school. If she's stuck in a class on her own without a teacher and simply told to get on with it, her education will suffer.

'I have said she can have the stud — that should be good enough for the school. It doesn't affect her work. This is taking things too far.

'She doesn't wear earrings — she has never had her ears pierced. It's not as though she is dripping in jewellery.

'There are girls in the sixth form who have their eyebrows and their belly buttons pierced.

'Nothing is being done about them. Nerissa is being singled out for no good reason. It's not fair.'

Nerissa, who also likes the Back Street Boys, said: 'None of my friends had a tongue stud. I wanted to be the first.

'It was like a prick from a needle when I had it done. Now I don't notice it. If I took it out, it would close up after 15 or 30 minutes.

'I think the school are making a big deal out of it. If it's good enough for Scary Spice, it's good enough for me.'

Yesterday Nerissa's parents were keeping her at home in Rothwell in protest.

Mr Dale, who has been head of Montsaye School, a comprehen-

Spice Girls' Mel B with her stud

sive with 1,100 pupils aged 11 to 18, for 16 years, defended his ruling.

'We have strict rules on wearing jewellery,' he said. 'Pupils are allowed one set of stud earrings and that is it.

'Safety is obviously one of our main concerns. We think this could be potentially dangerous.

'I haven't seen it myself — I'm not in the habit of asking children to stick their tongues out at me.

'Nerissa's mother has been into school and said that she will take responsibility for it, but I'm afraid rules are rules.'

Read and discuss

In the exam, you may be asked to comment on the way paragraphs are used in a newspaper article. In order to do this successfully, it is important to understand how journalists use paragraphs and why they use them in the way they do.

What comments would you make on the use of paragraphs in the *Daily Mail* article: 'Lesson Ban on Girl Who Made Herself Look Really Scary'? The following questions might help to get you started:

▶ How do the paragraphs in this article differ from the rules that you have learned about paragraphing?
▶ What is the average number of sentences per paragraph in the article?
▶ How are the essential facts of the report divided between the paragraphs?
▶ How does the paragraph structure help to keep the reader's attention? Think about the length of each paragraph and the number of paragraphs in the article.

Write

1 The *Daily Mail* article consists of 22 paragraphs. Restructure it to reduce the number of paragraphs to six. You don't have to rewrite the article; just look for ways of joining a number of short paragraphs to make successful longer ones.

2 Then write out the opening and closing sentences of each of your six new paragraphs.

3 Finally, write a few lines about each new paragraph to explain how it contributes to the development of the story. How closely does your restructured article follow the 'normal' rules on paragraphs?

Homework

1 Find a news report in a broadsheet newspaper, cut it out and stick it on a larger piece of paper to create a margin on all sides.

2 In the margin, **either** write notes to show what each paragraph contributes to the development of the story **or** give each paragraph a topic heading.

3 How do the paragraphs in the broadsheet news story differ from those in the tabloid news story?

Sentences

Learning aims

▶ To be able to identify some of the common **sentence structures** used by journalists.

▶ To understand why those structures are frequently used.

Facts

▶ Writers change their sentence structure according to the kind of writing they want to produce and the audience for whom they are writing.

▶ Journalists have developed recognizable sentence structure patterns; this is especially noticeable in tabloid journalism, but can also be seen in many broadsheets.

▶ Most journalists follow the golden rule of journalism, that is, always try to answer the five Ws:

▶ Who is involved?

▶ What happened?

▶ When did it happen?

▶ Where did it happen?

▶ Why did it happen?

Their sentence structure will often reflect this rule.

The article on page 34 appeared in the *Mirror* on 30 July, 1998.

I'VE BEEN A MITE LUCKY

NEEDLE SHARP: (left)
Cave dweller stalagmite

ON THE MEND: (right)
John yesterday, reliving his nightmare plunge.

By STEVE ATKINSON and MARK DOWDNEY

Brit caver John survives 6-hour ordeal impaled on a stalagmite

A BRITISH potholer lay in agony for six hours after a 30-foot plunge left him impaled on a stalagmite deep underground.

John Vale, 28, told yesterday how blood poured from his body with the sharp rock embedded in his back.

As he slipped in and out of consciousness his only company was the host of bugs and spiders in his cave tomb.

But after 90 minutes of surgery on his cracked pelvis and other wounds, John was just counting his blessings to be alive last night.

He said: 'I knew I was in serious trouble and losing a lot of blood but there was nothing I could do but hang on. I have to admit I was pretty scared.'

John from Derby, and caver pal Phil Galbraith, 24, were exploring New Zealand's spectacular Waitomo Caves 50 miles from Hamilton.

The pair, both working as holiday chefs at a nearby ski resort, had been climbing down for 20 minutes when John fell.

He said: 'The rocks were getting increasingly wet and slippery and suddenly I just lost my grip and fell. I didn't have time to scream — I just felt a nasty jab in my back as I fell on to something in the stream below.

'I couldn't move and as soon as I felt the blood from my cracked pelvis and lower back I knew I was in serious trouble, though I'd also had a very lucky escape.

'Phil, who had a first aid kit on him, climbed down to me and patched me up. God knows what I would have done if he hadn't have been with me.'

But New Zealander Phil had to leave his friend and retrace their steps to raise the alarm.

And it was a total of six hours before a doctor and rescue team, riding the subterranean tunnels on small craft, could reach him.

Dr Uresh Naidu said: 'We waded, crawled and crouched in waist-deep water with walls covered in sharp limestone while carrying our equipment — it was very cumbersome.'

Guide Charlene Beckett, 25, held bandages in place over a puncture wound near his kidney for 75 minutes to staunch the blood. Then his stretcher was threaded back out through the caves in a tortuous four-hour operation.

John said: 'Charlene was amazing and the whole team were absolutely brilliant.'

He added: 'It was a nasty tumble. But the caves were beautiful — and I can't wait to get back.'

I'VE BEEN A MITE LUCKY

NEEDLE SHARP: (left)
Cave dweller stalagmite

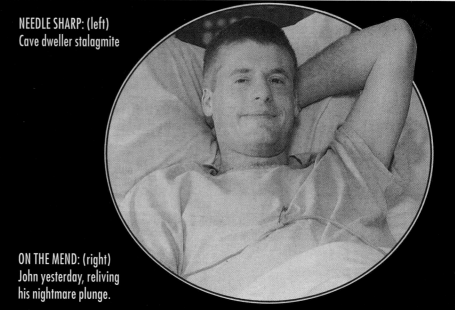

ON THE MEND: (right)
John yesterday, reliving
his nightmare plunge.

By STEVE ATKINSON and
MARK DOWDNEY

Brit caver John survives 6-hour ordeal impaled on a stalagmite

1 A BRITISH potholer lay in agony for six hours after a 30-foot plunge left him impaled on a stalagmite deep underground.

1 John Vale, 28, told yesterday how blood poured from his body with the sharp rock embedded in his back.

2 As he slipped in and out of **3** consciousness his only company was the host of bugs and spiders in his cave tomb.

But after 90 minutes of surgery on his cracked pelvis and other wounds, John was just counting his blessings to be alive last night.

He said: 'I knew I was in serious trouble and losing a lot of blood but **4** there was nothing I could do but hang on. I have to admit I was pretty scared.'

John from Derby, and caver pal Phil Galbraith, 24, were exploring New Zealand's spectacular Waitomo Caves 50 miles from Hamilton.

The pair, both working as holiday chefs at a nearby ski resort, had been climbing down for 20 minutes when John fell.

He said: 'The rocks were getting increasingly wet and slippery and suddenly I just lost my grip and fell. I didn't have time to scream — I just felt a nasty jab in my back as I fell on to something in the stream below.

'I couldn't move and as soon as I felt the blood from my cracked pelvis and lower back I knew I was in serious trouble, though I'd also had a very lucky escape.

'Phil, who had a first aid kit on him, climbed down to me and patched me up. God knows what I would have done if he hadn't have been with me.'

6 But New Zealander Phil had to leave his friend and retrace their steps to raise the alarm.

6 And it was a total of six hours before a doctor and rescue team, riding the subterranean tunnels on small craft, could reach him.

Dr Uresh Naidu said: 'We waded, crawled and crouched in waist-deep water with walls covered in sharp limestone while carrying our equipment — it was very cumbersome.'

Guide Charlene Beckett, 25, held bandages in place over a puncture wound near his kidney for 75 minutes to staunch the blood. Then his stretcher was threaded back out through the caves in a tortuous four-hour operation.

John said: 'Charlene was amazing and the whole team were absolutely brilliant.'

He added: 'It was a nasty tumble. But the caves were beautiful — and I can't wait to get back.'

The numbered handwritten notes below explain the different types of sentence structure used in the article on page 34. These are typical examples of sentence structure used by journalists in this kind of newspaper.

The grammar notes which follow will remind you of the meanings of some of the grammatical terms.

Grammar notes

1 *Many sentences begin with the subject and the main clause.*

The **subject** of the sentence is what the sentence is about: the person who is 'doing' or 'being' the action of the verb. A **clause** is a part of a sentence (and may be a complete sentence). It contains a subject and a verb.

2 *When a sentence begins with a subordinate clause it is usually a short one so that you don't lose sight of the real subject.*

Some sentences have a **main clause** and a **subordinate (or dependent) clause**, joined by a **conjunction**. The **main clause** would make sense if it stood on its own without the rest of the sentence. The **subordinate clause** needs the main clause and could not make sense on its own.

3 *A complex sentence consisting of a main clause and an adverbial clause (in either order) is a common structure.*

A **complex sentence** is one which contains a **main clause** and one or more **subordinate clauses**. Often the subordinate clause will come first.

An **adverbial clause** is a common type of **subordinate clause**. It tells us more about the meaning of the **verb** in the **main clause**. It is introduced by **conjunctions** such as 'although', 'after', 'because', 'despite', 'when', 'whenever', 'where', 'since', 'as'.

4 *Coordinated sentences are also common.*

In a **coordinated sentence**, two or more **main clauses** are joined by 'or', 'and' or 'but'.

5 *Direct speech is usually introduced by 'He said:' etc., rather than followed by it as in fiction.*

6 *Sentence conjunctions such as 'But' or 'And' are frequently used as paragraph connectives.*

In other kinds of writing, **paragraphs** are linked to one another by **connectives** such as 'however', 'in fact', 'as well as this'.

Read and discuss

In the exam, you might be asked to show what techniques a journalist has used in writing a report of a news item. Look carefully again at each of the six features of sentence structure highlighted on the news article 'I've Been a Mite Lucky' on page 34 and the handwritten explanations on page 35. Then try to answer the following questions. While doing so, don't forget the golden rule of journalism which shapes every article – the five Ws:
Who? What? When? Where? Why?

1 What is the effect of beginning most sentences with the subject?

2 Why do journalists often use a main clause with an adverbial clause?

3 Why are there so many coordinated sentences?

4 Why do so many new paragraphs start with conjunctions?

5 Why do you think these examples and the others highlighted by the handwritten notes on page 35 have become common features of journalism?

Write

Pick an exciting news story and write four or five paragraphs of an article in tabloid style, following the paragraph and sentence conventions that you have learned about here and in Unit 6.

Homework

1 Find a tabloid news article, cut it out and stick it on a larger piece of paper to create a margin on all sides.

2 Using the examples highlighted on page 34-35 as a guide, make notes in the margin to show some of the sentence features in your chosen article.

Quotation and reported comment

Learning aims

▶ To identify the purposes for which **quotations** and **reported comments** are used.

▶ To understand the conventions of **direct speech layout** in newspaper articles.

Facts

▶ Quotation and reported comments are used frequently in newspaper reporting and feature writing.

▶ Quotations serve a variety of purposes, such as:
  ▶ they help the reader relate to the people in the story
  ▶ they add authority, especially when spoken by an 'expert'
  ▶ they make links with issues wider than the reported story.

▶ There are a number of conventions to follow when using quotation (direct speech) and reported (indirect) speech (see page 39).

This article appeared in the *Daily Mail* on 25 September, 1998. It shows how quotations and reported comments can be used in a news report to support a particular viewpoint.

World's first limb transplant for man with severed forearm

MY MIRACLE NEW HAND

From LESLEY HUSSELL in Lyon and RICHARD SHEARS in Sydney

10 THE world's first hand transplant patient sat up in his hospital bed last night and said: 'It's a miracle.' 1

10 Clint Hallam, who lost his hand and part of his forearm 14 years ago, was speaking after a remarkable 12-hour operation in which a British surgeon played a leading role.

He received his new limb from a man left fatally brain-damaged after an accident.

The operation is seen as the biggest breakthrough in such surgery since the first heart transplant 31 years ago.

Doctors have been re-attaching limbs for years but have been unwilling to transplant limbs from another person.

The body rejects an organ or limb from somebody else and powerful drugs have to be used to overcome the problem, usually for life and with serious side effects.

The development of revolutionary anti-rejection drugs with fewer side effects has made operations such as that on Mr Hallam possible.

His astonishing operation will open the way for patients to be fitted with the feet, full arms or legs of others, one of the surgery team said last night.

It may also restart the debate over the ethics of such advances.

There will be concern that doctors might want to keep patients alive by artificial means, despite a family's wishes, so that they can keep a body 'fresh' for use in such operations.

2

Last night, as he recovered in the Edouard Herriot hospital in the French city of Lyon, Mr Hallam spoke of his excitement at the prospect of again having the use of a right arm and hand.

'I'm very, very tired but extremely happy,' said 10 the 48-year-old Australian. 'I've been waiting a long time and it's absolutely wonderful. 8

'The next step is being able to move my new hand. Then there will be so many things to look forward to.

9 'Hugging my wife Daphne and my four children is definitely top of the list. It'll be good to play the piano again as well.'

11 British professor Nadey Hakim said Mr Hallam, who lost the limb in a chainsaw accident in a prison workshop while serving time for theft, wept with joy when he saw his new hand.

3 'He pushed for this operation for many, many years but he had to find a doctor who would believe in him,' he said.

'It is a daring thing to do because it is not like a heart transplant where the patient will die otherwise.

7 'Mr Hallam was alive and there was no medical urgency. But he wanted a new arm and that's what he's got. He's doing well and he's in excellent spirits.'

Doctors are cautiously confident of complete success, and say he should have some feeling in his 4 hand over the next 48 hours.

Eventually he should be able to reach and grip, although it will take months to gain full use and

when he touches himself it will feel like someone else doing it.

The incredible surgery will bring hope to millions of amputees, including babies born with limbs missing, people with congenital defects and those with disfiguring injuries.

The transplant team was led by Professor Jean-Michel Dubernard, with surgeons from Italy, Australia and France.

He said afterwards: 'It went very well and we are pleased with the way the hand took.'

10 When Mr Hallam, from Perth, lost his hand 14 years ago surgeons were able to reattach it, but the operation was not a success.

Frustrated at being unable to hold his wife, play with his children or practise the piano, he had the hand removed and began his quest for some form of medical advancement to end his pain. Last night one of the surgical team, Frenchman Xavier Martin said: 'If this one works, the way is open for many more developments.

'Arm transplants should become possible, as well 5 as fingers, toes, feet and whole legs.

'In the future I would not even rule out the possibility of head transplants once techniques have been developed further. Anything is possible. But heads certainly raise ethical questions.'

Mr Hallam's mental reaction to having someone else's hand would be monitored by a psychiatrist, he added.

'When people have internal organ transplants like a liver, they often have strange feelings because they have something foreign in their bodies. They sometimes say they feel as though they have a baby inside them.

'The hand is obviously more visible. We'll have to see what the reaction is. But the patient showed no particular anxiety before the operation.'

The operation was carried out under France's public health system, in which transplants are free.

Plastic surgeon Stewart Watson, who frequently re-attaches severed hands and fingers at Withington Hospital in Manchester said: 'It's what we've been waiting for. We would love to be doing it.

'The techniques for doing hand transplants are well-established and in some ways it should be even easier than replanting a hand, which is something we do fairly regularly, since you would have time to prepare for it.' 6

The notes under the 'Purposes' heading explain why a particular quotation or comment has been used.

The notes under the 'Conventions' heading explain how the quotation or comment is presented on the page and how it fits in with the rest of the narrative.

Purposes

1 The quotation is used as part of a dramatic intro – it also introduces the feelings of the story's 'hero'

2 This word is placed in inverted commas to show that this is somebody else's term, and not necessarily approved of by the writer

3 The professor is a major 'player' in the story; in addition his comments add 'authority'

4 Further unnamed 'doctors' add authority, but are not quoted 'verbatim' (word-for-word)

5 A quotation from a different surgeon is used to raise wider issues

6 This quotation serves two purposes – it concludes the report by looking to the future and reinforces the 'home' perspective on a foreign story

Conventions

7 Use of single speech marks

8 If the quotation extends into another paragraph, speech marks are not closed, but are 're-opened'

9 The speaker's words don't sound quite like 'real' speech; they have been 'tidied up' for two reasons – to fit the story's particular 'angle' and to be easily digested by the reader

10 Different ways are found in which to identify Clint Hallam for two reasons – to avoid repetition and to highlight a different aspect of him

11 Reported speech is often used to lead into quotation

Read and discuss

Journalists will use the facts and quoted comments in their reports in order to put over a particular viewpoint. You may be asked to comment on this important feature of newspaper writing in the exam. The *Daily Mail* article 'My Miracle New Hand' takes a positive view of the operation to give Clint Hallam a new hand and uses the quotations to support that view.

1 Study the report again and discuss how a careful selection of the **same** quotations might be used in an article which was unhappy about the idea of transplants like this. (See the reference in the article to 'the debate over the ethics of such advances'.)

2 Then note down which quotations from the article might be selected and how they could be used in a new article to give a negative 'spin' to the story.

3 Finally, to bring this new 'angle' to life, improvise a radio debate in which a presenter interviews a selection of the doctors quoted in the article. In their responses, the doctors use the quotations you have highlighted to attack the operation.

Write

This short article, which appeared in the *Times* on 30 July 1998, shows how quotations can be used to tell most of the story.
► The first paragraph introduces the story.
► A quotation from the owner then takes up the story.
► The vet continues, adding a personal viewpoint.
► The story concludes with two light-hearted comments.

Tom loses to Jerry as mouse bites cat

by Paul Wilkinson

A TOM cat was suffering from wounded pride yesterday after being bitten by a 4in mouse. Widget, a pedigree lilac burmese, had been toying with his latest catch in Hexham, Northumberland, but then suddenly ran in from the garden with a cut neck.

'The mouse had leapt up and given him a nasty bite,' said Marion Robinson, owner of 15-month-old Widget.

'When I telephoned our vet and told her why I needed to bring Widget to the surgery, she burst out laughing.'

Christine Shield, the vet, said: 'I did laugh. In all my years as a vet I have never heard that one before. The mouse had left a puncture mark on his throat. I gave him an antibiotic jab. His pride was probably more hurt than anything else. I'm sure he will be a bit quicker the next time.'

Using this as your model, draft a similar short article in which the quotations drive the story forward.

Homework

1 Find a news report which uses lots of direct and indirect speech similar to the one about the hand transplant. Cut it out and stick it on a larger piece of paper to create a margin on all sides.

2 Using the headings 'Purposes' and 'Conventions', make notes in the margin and use arrows to identify the ways in which quotations and reported speech have been used. You may find it helpful to look back to the lists on page 39.

Register

Learning aims

▸ To understand the concept of **register**.
▸ To identify the **informal register** commonly used in tabloids and occasionally in broadsheet journalism.

Facts

▸ Register is the term given to the style of language which seems to suit a particular situation or social context or a certain kind of subject-matter.
▸ Different kinds of writing, appearing in different publications, for different audiences, will be written in different registers (see computer magazines, medical journals, etc.).
▸ The most noticeable difference in registers is between
  ▸ **informal** – used, for example, in letters to friends, and
  ▸ **formal** – used in most writing aimed at a wider public.
▸ Tabloid newspapers will often deliberately use an informal register (and occasionally a **colloquial** register - one closer to everyday speech), in preference to the more formal register normally used by broadsheets in their main news stories.
▸ Broadsheets also sometimes use this informal register in articles that they consider less serious or less 'weighty'.
▸ Informal register often contains examples of 'inverted snobbery', where the writer deliberately mocks anything it considers 'posh' or 'intellectual', as a way of getting on the reader's side.

Tabloid informal register can be seen in a number of ways. Look at the article 'Why Men and Women Should Stop Trying to be More Like Each Other and Enjoy Being ... Worlds Apart' on page 42.

Why men and women should stop trying to be more like each other and enjoy being ...
WORLDS APART

By KATHERINE MacALISTER

SHE may not be the best role model in the world when it comes to offering advice on marital problems, but Fergie can certainly cut it when it comes to striking deals.

So it came as no surprise to anyone to learn yesterday what her latest advance was reportedly in the £500,000 ballpark. What may be a little more than eyebrow-raising is that she is choosing to write about how to deal with man trouble.

But if Fergie isn't your first choice for marriage guidance counsellor, there's a whole bunch of people in Oxford this week who are regarded as some of the world's leading experts in exactly that field.

And the message from the top is: If your marriage is going through a rough patch, fear not.

Although the experts — who are meeting all week at St Catherine's College — may not be concentrating on your particular problem, their conference could benefit us all.

The billion-dollar question taxing the relationship gurus at the moment is this: Are men and women different?

Why men and women should stop trying to be more like each other and enjoy being ...
WORLDS APART

By KATHERINE MacALISTER

1 SHE may not be the best role model in the world when it comes to offering advice on marital problems, but **3** Fergie **2** can certainly cut it when it comes to striking deals.

So it came as no surprise to anyone to learn yesterday that her latest advance was reportedly in the £500,000 **4** ballpark. What may be a little more than eyebrow-raising **5** is that she is choosing to write about how to deal with man trouble. **6**

But if Fergie isn't your first choice for marriage guidance counsellor, there's a whole **7** bunch of people in Oxford this week who are regarded as some of the world's leading experts in exactly that field.

And the message from the top is: If your marriage is going through a rough patch, fear not. **8**

Although the experts — who are meeting all week at St Catherine's College — may not be concentrating on your particular problem, their conference could benefit us all. **9** **10**

The billion-dollar question taxing the relationship gurus at the moment is this: Are men and women different?

The numbered handwritten notes below relate to the numbers on the news article above.

1 Chatty, informal opening

2 Use of her popular nickname, rather than her official title

3 Slang expression designed to make the writer seem fashionable

4 An American borrowing, now a cliché of finance people

5 Colloquialism intended as a witty alternative to 'surprising'

6 The language of popular magazines

7 Colloquialism perhaps designed to mock the rather pompous 'world's leading experts'

8 Jokey address to the reader

9 Cliché which originated years ago in television quiz shows

10 Fashionable alternative to 'experts'

Read and discuss

Being able to identify the register of an article and comment upon its features, is a useful skill for the exam.

1 Look back at the articles 'Lesson Ban on Girl Who Made Herself Look Really Scary' in Unit 6 and 'I've Been a Mite Lucky' in Unit 7.

2 Choose some extracts or paragraphs from the articles and make notes on how they might be redrafted into an even more informal register.

3 Then compare your suggestions with other people.

Write

Redraft 'Worlds Apart' in a formal register, as it might appear as a serious news item in a broadsheet newspaper.

Homework

1 Select an appropriate tabloid article, cut it out and stick it on a larger piece of paper to create a margin on all sides.

2 Using the handwritten notes on page 42 as a guide, make notes in the margin and use arrows to highlight examples of informal register in your chosen report.

Stock expressions

Learning aims	▶ To be able to identify and discuss the effect of journalistic **stock expressions**. ▶ To understand and use the concepts of **lexis** and **syntax** when discussing the language of newspapers.
Facts	▶ News journalists are very aware that most of their writing has to be 　▶ up-to-the-minute 　▶ drafted very quickly to meet a deadline 　▶ written for an audience which is easily distracted (because they are travelling to work, for example, or snatching a ten-minute break at lunchtime). They therefore often choose language which is familiar or will capture the reader's interest immediately. ▶ Examples of attention-grabbing language include **punning headlines** and **journalese shorthand** (described in Unit 4), and the use of a punchy **intro** (see Unit 5). But there are other features of newspaper writing which serve similar purposes; some are to do with vocabulary (or **lexis**), others with grammar and phrasing (or **syntax**).

Lexis

Stock expressions

When a journalist describes an old lady as 'white-haired' or a hero as 'plucky', they are using a stock expression, a familiar phrase which will have an immediate and predictable impact upon the reader. Usually the adjective will have **connotations** (suggested meanings) which the reader is expected to pick up. For example, 'white-haired' suggests that the old lady is sweet and defenceless.

Read and discuss

1 Match up the stock adjective in the left-hand column on page 45 with its noun in the right-hand column and write out the complete phrase.

2 Then discuss the following:
▶ the connotations the resulting phrase would have
▶ the kind of article you might expect to find it in
▶ the effect a writer might hope to gain by using it.

Adjectives	Nouns
distinguished	ex-lover
vexed	widow
dishy (or stunning)	problem
broken-hearted	Catholic
grieving	surgeon
bored	staff
devout	question
trained	housewife
knotty	model

3 Look at the list of words below.

the animal welfare lobby
the party faithful
the rat race
it has become a mecca for...
their love-nest
a street of shame

▶ What does each of these stock expressions mean?
▶ In what context or situation might each be used?
▶ What connotations might each phrase have?

Emotive language

Emotive and romantic words add colour and are easily slotted into the sentence. Like other stock expressions, they carry connotations which the reader is expected to pick up. For example, almost any kind of bad experience becomes an 'agony', 'anguish', 'torture', 'nightmare', 'terror' or 'ordeal'; while people's hopes are 'dreams' or 'fantasies'.

Read and discuss

The first visit of Nelson Mandela to this country as President of South Africa was inevitably labelled 'historic'.

1 Discuss what kind of event or incident each of the following stock emotive adjectives might be used to describe:

horrifying	tragic	heart-warming
heart-stopping	shattering	staggering
scandalous	devastating	cataclysmic
moving	disastrous	

2 Compare your answers with other people.

Special uses of words

Several features of language use are particularly common to journalism. They include:

- ▶ **conversions** (e.g. nouns used as verbs, such as 'to foreground' an issue)
- ▶ **attributives** (e.g. nouns qualifying other nouns, as in 'death' ride, 'fun' dome)
- ▶ **compounds** (e.g. 'player-manager', 'model-turned-actress')
- ▶ **rhyme pairs** or **reduplicatives** (e.g. rhymes, such as 'jet-set', 'culture-vulture')
- ▶ **archaisms** (e.g. old-fashioned words such as 'agog', 'foe', 'scribe')
- ▶ **neologisms** (expressions which are invented by journalists and then enter the spoken language, such as 'lookalike', 'yuppie')

Read and discuss

Using the examples outlined above, decide which category each of the following belongs to:

spin-doctor	to 'access' information	brain-drain
slay	mercy dash	kiss-and-tell

Syntax

Newspaper writing is often identifiable because of the particular ways it uses **modification** (the adding of adjectives to nouns or adverbs to verbs). For example, it is common to find strings of adjectives and attributive nouns attached to a person's name. For example: 'Liverpool-born ex-Beatle George Harrison...' or 'Margaret Thatcher, ex-Premier, "Iron Lady" of British politics...'

Read and discuss

1 Think up some suitable strings of adjectives and attributive nouns, to modify the name of any well known figure from history, or any current celebrity.

2 Challenge your partner to work out who the person is from the modification you have chosen.

Write

Write a short newspaper article which includes examples of the stock phrases and expressions featured in this unit.

Homework

1 Look through a selection of newspapers and find further examples of the language features discussed in this unit.

2 Then using what you have learned from Units 4 to 10, write an article entitled 'The Language of Newspapers'.

Who are the advertisers?

Learning aims	▶ To become aware of the variety of different **bodies** involved in print-media advertising and the different **purposes** for which they advertise.
Facts	▶ Most advertisements are trying to sell a **product**. This might be a commercial product (such as Persil or Pepsi-Cola) or a financial service (such as Barclays Bank or Bradford & Bingley Building Society).
	▶ For an increasing number of advertisements these days, the 'product' is a charity (such as Oxfam) or a campaign (see Action for Wildlife leaflet on page 52).
	▶ There are also government-supported organizations (such as the Health Education Authority), who issue public service or public information leaflets. These are also a form of advertising because their aims are usually to inform and to persuade.

Commercial companies selling goods

The following advertisements are examples from eight different types of advertiser.

Shopping centres

Commercial companies selling an experience

Insurance companies

SAGA PRIVATE HEALTHCARE PLAN

Automatic acceptance for prompt medical attention if you are 50 or over

Don't Let Time Pass You By

Emma rocks the boat

ENJOY ALL THE BENEFITS OF PRIVATE MEDICAL INSURANCE

SAGA INSURANCE SERVICES

Banks

Mortgage advice wherever and whenever you want.

♻ NatWest
More than just a bank

Every day Nyanyiik has to drink water through a filter pipe **or more worms will grow inside her**

Eleven year old Nyanyiik Magac lives in southern Sudan in Africa.

In her village the only drinking water is filthy and often contains the eggs of the Guinea worm. These eggs hatch and grow up to one metre in length (like the worm shown on this page) and live in the intestines. After a year the worms break through the body, usually out of the legs or feet, causing unbelievable pain. Often the victims are unable to work or plant crops, which can lead to food shortages.

Nyanyiik has already suffered [...] worms, and it was removed [...] Now she has another Gui[...]

❝ I'm scared because I know there's another worm in my foot which still has to come out and I remember how painful this was last time ❞

To avoid more Guinea worm eggs entering her body, Nyanyiik has to drink water through a filter pipe, which is shared by several families.

Charities

irs in your life takes to help e like Nyanyiik

WORLD VISION
orldvision.org.uk
24 HOUR FAMINE

Commercial companies offering a service

Today RAC membership Tomorrow the world
Join the RAC and take off with up to 360 AIR MILES awards

Special offer inside for existing RAC Members

0800 029 029

RAC

Government-funded agencies

Take ecstasy and you're experimenting on yourself.

There's no such thing as a safe E.
You just don't know what the cocktail of chemicals is and even if you did, you wouldn't know what the long term effects are because no one does – yet. Current evidence suggests it could cause depression, personality change and memory loss.
For more information or just a talk, [...] confidence on 0800 77 66 00 and **know the score.**

national drugs helpline
0800 77 66 00

Read and discuss

In your exam, you may need to comment on where an advertisement comes from; for example, a commercial company, a charity or a government-funded agency.

1 Choose six of the eight categories shown on pages 48-49.

2 For each category, discuss other examples of print-media advertisements that you have seen which you think are particularly effective.

Sometimes two different advertisers will join forces on a combined advertisement. Here is an example.

Help put wildlife back into our wetlands

Help raise £1 million - and it needn't cost you a penny.

Our wetlands are in danger. Drainage, agriculture, water abstraction and lack of management are all threatening these vital habitats – and their birds. Once common waders like curlew, redshank and lapwing are in decline. Geese, ducks and birds of prey are losing vital feeding grounds. And rare species like the bittern could soon be lost altogether.

We need to act fast. We must acquire land, create and restore wetlands, introduce wildlife-friendly management techniques, and change land use. But to do that, we need your help.

Help save wetlands when you spend

The RSPB Visa card could raise £1 million for wetlands in danger over the next three years. And you could help.

The Co-operative Bank will give £10 to our wetlands in danger campaign when you open an account. It will give another £2.50 if your card is being used six months later – and a further 25p for every £100 you spend using the card.

The first and only 100% biodegradable credit card

The RSPB Visa Card is made from a natural, biodegradable material called Biopol, produced from plant extracts. That makes the RSPB Visa Card the world's only 100% environmentally friendly credit card.

You'll benefit too

The RSPB Visa card offers you significant benefits too. Like a guarantee never to charge you an annual fee, a promise to match your existing credit limit, and competitive interest rates.

Why not find out more – and see how you can help wetlands in danger at no extra cost to you?

Read and discuss

1 Look at the magazine advertisement on page 50 and identify the two organizations in partnership in the advertisement.

2 Identify the commercial product and discuss what the aims of the charity are.

3 Then discuss why the two groups might have considered it a good idea to advertise jointly in this way.

Write

Think of two print-media advertisements, one from a commercial company, one from a charity (you could use examples from pages 48-49 or find ones in later units) and write to the companies concerned giving your opinions on how successful their advertisements are.

Write

1 Choose a charity and a commercial company who might be able to advertise jointly as the organizations in the advertisement on page 50 have done.

2 Explain why they might make successful advertising partners, and sketch out a rough version of the resulting advertisement, paying attention to both the image and the copy.

Homework

1 Choose three different publications (for example, a broadsheet newspaper, a magazine and a periodical such as the *Radio Times*) which contain advertisements.

2 Make a list of the different organizations which advertise in each one and what they advertise.

3 Try to put each organization into one of the eight categories outlined on pages 48-49. Don't worry if some don't seem to fit.

4 Then make notes on the following:
   ▶ Which of the eight categories seem to be advertising most frequently in each publication?
   ▶ Which of them least frequently?
   ▶ Are there advertisements which do not fit easily into one of the eight categories?
   ▶ Do certain advertisers appear in particular publications?

Advertising and the print media

Learning aims

> ▸ To become familiar with the different kinds of **printed media** used by organizations to **advertise** their products or cause.

Facts

> ▸ Sound and visual media, such as radio, television, cinema, video, and the internet are well-used by advertisers. However, advertisers also rely heavily on 'selling' their product through the various forms of printed media.

> ▸ According to language specialist David Crystal, there are lots of places in which advertisers can 'sell' their product or message. These include: billboards, book jackets, bookmarks, carrier bags, catalogues, circulars, flyers, handbills, inserts, labels, special merchandise (such as cups, pens and T-shirts), notices, placards, posters, price tags, programmes, samples, sandwich boards, sportswear, showcards, signs, tickets, tourism brochures, media trailers, vehicle sides, wrapping paper, and classified pages in telephone books.

> ▸ A great deal of print advertising also comes through our letterboxes in the form of direct mail (sometimes known as 'junk mail').

The exam concentrates on the printed media, and particularly on advertising in newspapers, magazines and leaflets. Here are some examples of the various types of advertisement that you might be asked to discuss and analyse.

Campaign LEAFLET

Commercial LEAFLET

reader offer

the **must-have** shirts from **Browns**

Commercial advertisement from a NEWSPAPER SUPPLEMENT ('The Times')

...s can ...otton ...gned ...ns of ...e of the most prestigious fashion shops in London. A plain white shirt is the essential fashion item this season, with all the top designers making the classic white shirt a feature of their collections.

The ladies' version is slightly fitted, has ...

...it measures

Charity advertisement from a PERIODICAL (the 'Radio Times')

ENABLED

Right now a disabled person:

(a) desperately needs your help.

(b) could be enabled by your donation.

I want more disabled people to benefit from the Leonard Cheshire service which enables Gillian to live independently. I want to change a life for the better, forever.

I enclose a donation of £10/£ ......

Name ....

Address ....

(RT2710) Postcode ....

Please make cheques payable to Leonard Cheshire Foundation. Return this coupon to: Leonard Cheshire, Freepost, SW5925, London, SW1P 4YY.

For information or to make a donation, call
0845 606 50 50

Creating opportunities with disabled people

LEONARD CHESHIRE

www.leonard-cheshire.org   Patron: Her Majesty The Queen
Registered charity no. 218186

the times magazine + Browns

I enclose a ...
The Times ...
Please write ...
cheques ...
Or debit my ...

No ...

Postcode ...

Expiry Date ...

Signature ...

...d me
...ntity of shirts required)

S (10) M (12) L (14) XL (16)

L (16) XL (16½)

Total

Send coupon ...
The Times ...
Browns shir...
PO Box 345...

Delivery within...
please return &...
refund. Offer s...

COVER GIRL

Commercial advertisement from a MAGAZINE ('Nineteen')

Life is complicated. Make-up shouldn't be.

Looking good has never been easier thanks to Cover Girl's Simply Powder Foundation. It covers like a liquid foundation, but it's a powder! So go on, give it a try, because your life may be complicated but your make-up shouldn't be.

...R GIRL

easy

Public information LEAFLET

Have YOU ever felt SLEEPY while DRIVING?

If your answer is YES, look inside...

RNID

It's **time** to test your hearing

10:00 Dentist

4:45 Hai...

11:30 Optician

THE ROYAL NATIONAL INSTITUTE FOR DEAF PEOPLE

Charity LEAFLET

Read and discuss

In pairs, look back at David Crystal's list of possible advertising spaces in the Facts section on page 52 and discuss the following:

▶ Has David Crystal left anything out?
▶ Which examples from David Crystal's list have you seen? Can you come up with any additional suggestions?
▶ In your opinion, which ones were most effective and why?

Write

1 Draw out a chart like the one below. Using the examples on pages 52-53, fill in the chart by adding
   ▶ the name of the product
   ▶ what category of advertising it falls into
   ▶ where it appears.

The first example has been done for you.

PLACE	PRODUCT	CATEGORY
magazine	Cover Girl make-up	commercial product
newspaper		
leaflet		

2 Then extend the chart by adding further examples of printed advertisements that you have seen in different places.

Homework

1 Find as many examples as you can of advertisements which you consider to be particularly effective from
   ▶ newspapers or magazines
   ▶ leaflets.

2 Make notes on the advantages of each of these two print media for advertising and keep them safe. You may find them useful in later units.

Target groups

Learning aims

▶ To become aware that advertisements are produced with particular **audiences** in mind.
▶ To understand the concept of **target groups**.

Facts

▶ 'Who is this advertising campaign to be aimed at?' This is a vital question for any advertising agency. Identifying the right audience is essential to producing a successful advertisement. This audience is usually referred to as the target group.
▶ Target groups are usually listed under three main headings: **gender**, **age** and **class**.
   ▶ Gender can be broken down into three sub-groups: male, female, male and female.
   ▶ Age is divided into five groups: up to 15, 16-24, 25-35, 36-55, over 55.
   ▶ Social class is categorized by six groups: A, B, C1, C2, D and E (see Facts section on page 8 for a definition of each).
▶ In more specialist publications (such as hobbies magazines or football fanzines) the target groups might be decided by
   ▶ special interest: for example, railway enthusiasts; sports fans; animal-lovers, etc.
   ▶ other characteristics (such as cultural background, etc).
▶ For many products the advertiser will have to consider all three major target group headings – gender, age and class – when deciding how to 'present' the advertisement.

The advertisement on page 56 for the Freemans catalogue was created with very specific target groups in mind.

GENDER: female —
the Freemans catalogue wants to
feature Miss Selfridge clothes
particularly in this ad

AGE: 16-24 — the ad will appear in
the young women's magazine
'Nineteen'

CLASS: C1, C2 and D — these are
fairly inexpensive clothes for young
women who are not earning a high
salary

Read and discuss

1 Look carefully at the three advertisements on page 57.
Discuss which target groups the advertisers had in mind when they
devised these advertisements. List these under the headings:
gender, age and class.

Follow the example below based on the Freemans advertisement.

GENDER	AGE	CLASS
females	16–24	C1, C2 and D

2 State the reasons behind your decisions and then compare your
judgements with other people.
Some points to bear in mind:
▶ for some advertisements, a particular target group will not be
especially relevant, or it will be very difficult to work out
▶ in some cases, there might be two quite different groups
targeted in the same advertisement (such as young children
and their parents).

Write

1 Look back through Units 11 and 12, and analyse a selection of the advertisements on these pages according to their target groups. You could also use examples collected as part of the Homework activity in Unit 12.

2 Draw a grid like the one below and enter your findings. The first one has been done for you.

PRODUCT	TARGET GROUP		
	gender	age	class
Futurescope	male and female	all ages	A, B, C1

3 Compare your findings with a partner and discuss which gender, age and class groups seem to be targeted more than others, and why this might be.

Homework

1 Imagine that you work for an advertising agency and you have been asked to provide a draft plan for three advertisements.

2 Using a format like the example below, outline briefly some initial ideas for advertising three products (of your own choice) with quite different target groups.

HOTSHOT design & advertising

CLIENT ....

PRODUCT ....

TARGET GROUPS

....

GENDER ....

AGE ....

CLASS ....

INITIAL IDEAS

....

....

Design

▶ To understand which **design features** are used in print-media advertising and how they contribute to the effectiveness of the advertisement.

Facts

▶ Advertisers are constantly having to think up new ways in which to make their advertisements eye-catching and effective.
▶ While there are some differences between advertisements (for example, black-and-white and colour), there are many design features which most full-page and leaflet advertisements have in common.
▶ The elements of a print-media advertisement which contribute to its effectiveness are:
   ▶ **visuals** – photographs, line drawings, etc.
   ▶ **graphics** – lettering, logos, etc.
   ▶ **copy** – the journalist's and ad-writer's word for written text.

The advertisement for the Brother fax on page 60 shows examples of the design features which you might need to comment on in your exam.

The new Brother Fax-930.
All your messages go where you go.

The new Brother Fax-930.
All your messages go where you go.

The Fax-930 Digital Phone and Fax Message Centre

London. Glasgow. Even as far as New York or Australia. Wherever you travel, the new Brother Fax-930 Digital Message Centre can relay your faxes and phone messages to you.

Simply call your Fax-930 and it will play your voice messages. Or punch in the number of a nearby fax machine and it will forward your faxes on.

Whether you're out of the office or even the country, you need never be out of touch.

CALL NOW ON 0845 60 60 626

F1 brother / Tyrrell

2000+ FUTURE PROOF

brother®

QUOTING REF: SM003   Local rate call

Brother U.K. Ltd., Audenshaw, Manchester M34 5JD.   Brother Industries Limited, Nagoya, Japan. sales@buk.brother.co.uk

The numbered notes here refer to the numbers on the Brother fax advertisement on the opposite page.

1 Witty, arresting IMAGE – designed to catch the eye as you skim through the magazine and amuse or puzzle you when you look at it closely

2 SLOGAN – easy to understand and remember

3 The PRODUCT ILLUSTRATION – here there is a second photograph of the product to show how attractive it is

4 The SIGNATURE LINE – a repetition of the product name so that it will be remembered

5 SYMBOL – to show sponsorship connection with Formula 1 motor-racing, a high-prestige activity

6 Attractive COLOURS – (all different shades of blue — a colour associated with restfulness and reliability) used to divide the advertisement into four sections

7 Clear, unfussy GRAPHICS – this kind of typeface gives it a modern rather than a traditional feel

8 The BODY COPY (main block of text) – here the copy is brief: just enough to convey the main selling point (that you can call in to hear your messages)

9 Prominent LOGO – easily recognized when next seen

10 CAPITALIZATION – to make the telephone number stand out from the rest of the copy

11 Variation in PRINT SIZE – product name and slogan biggest; advertising copy smallest

12 Availability clearly stated as the final information in a bar across the bottom

Images

A powerful image will often be the centre point of an effective advertisement, as these two examples show.

Hawkshead Exclusive.
Buy the boots for only £29 and the socks are free.

The plain, unfussy presentation is designed to suit the product and the type of customer (see Unit 4)

Here the product is shown clearly, prominently and attractively

Comparing the mobile phone with a pair of glasses emphasizes its compactness, and there is also a link with 'vision' (meaning 'inventiveness') on the inside lid

Here in the Lake District we know a thing or two about walking, and we go out of our way to give real value for money.

That's why we're so pleased with our Hawkshead boot. It has a chunky treaded sole for a sure grip over rough terrain, and a contoured insole which helps shape the arch and cradle the foot.

The uppers are just as well thought out, made from a combination of supple Cordura® fabric and scuff resistant suede, and there's extra padding at the ankle and tongue for all round support.

At only £29 they were hard to beat for value, and with a free pair of wool-rich walking socks with every order, we're sure you'll feel even more comfortably off.

PATH APPEAL
For every pair of boots sold in this appeal we will donate £1 to the Lake District National Park to carry out vital work to stop erosion of the Lake District's upland paths.

DELIVERY
Please allow up to seven working days for your order to be delivered.
Next day delivery is available throughout most of the UK for a small additional charge £3.95 (plus Postage and Packing) on all telephone orders made before 12pm, Monday to Friday.

GUARANTEE
We have a no nonsense guarantee. If you are n...

HAWKSHEAD, WORKING IN PARTNERSHIP WITH THE LAKE DIS...

Hawkshead·Coniston·Windsor·Ambleside·Sheffield·Skipton·Stratford upon Avon·Bristol·...

A simple advertisement like this with virtually no copy is designed to make people feel that the company must be very confident and doesn't need to persuade you in words

NOKIA
8810

NOKIA
CONNECTING PEOPLE

Read and discuss

A major reason for including an image in an advertisement is to show the potential buyer what the product looks like.

1 Discuss the different choices of image made by the two advertisers on page 62.
   ▶ Why have they made this choice?
   ▶ Is it successful?

2 For a variety of reasons, however, many companies choose not to have a product illustration, but opt for an image which will serve quite a different purpose. Can you think of any examples of advertisements which you have seen in magazines and on billboards which do not show the product or even mention the product's name?
   ▶ Why do some companies or organizations do this?
   ▶ What is the impact of this kind of advert on the customer?

Write

1 Sketch out a magazine advertisement for a product of your own choice.

2 Include as many of the design features as possible outlined in the numbered handwritten notes for the Brother fax advertisement (see pages 60-61).

3 Then write a few lines to explain the effect you hope each design feature will have.

Homework

1 Collect a variety of magazine advertisements which make effective use of either striking images and/or graphics and typefaces.

2 Look through them for examples of the 12 design features highlighted on the Brother fax advertisement on page 60.

3 Circle or highlight each feature and write a few notes about why it is effective.

Combining visuals and copy

Learning aims	▶ To understand how advertisers combine **visuals** and **copy** for particular effects.
Facts	▶ Advertisements such as those found in the 'classified' section of the newspaper, or those for individual jobs, for example, tend to have no visuals at all (except perhaps for a company logo). At the other extreme, there are some advertisements which consist purely of visuals – perhaps a single photographic image – and do not even include the product name.
	▶ Most print-media advertisements, however, consist of some combination of visuals and copy.

The leaflet opposite, from British Gas, encourages customers to install new central heating systems. It is designed to catch the householder's attention in competition with dozens of similar 'promotions' (selling campaigns) which come through the letterbox . To do this it combines visuals and copy in a very effective way.

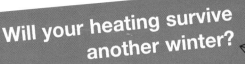

Will your heating survive another winter?

Spread the cost of new central heating with **interest-free credit***

OR buy now, pay in six months†

Plus the option to spread repayments over 1–5 years APR 26%†

British Gas Services

Front cover of leaflet

Alarmist opening question, offered like 'bait' to catch the reader's attention

Very simple copy on the front page, outlining only the main points of the offer

Blues throughout the front cover — cold colours to add to the message about winter

Witty, slightly bizarre image to catch the reader's attention

All the copy is 'reversed out' – that is, white letters on a coloured background

First page inside

Clear identifiable logo

Use of wordplay (in this case a 'paradox')

A similar bizarre illustration (the parrot is now in holiday clothes!) matches the one on the front cover, but is now in warm colours (even the perch has become yellower)

Copy expands on the alarmist headline message of the front cover and introduces the offer

Bullet points used to state the details of the offer as clearly as possible

The two most crucial features of the deal are in a larger type and enclosed in 'cartouches' (boxes with curved ends)

Clear simple style of type throughout

Chill out with new central heating

It's coming up to that time of year again. Frost, snow, icy rain … it's all part of the great British weather. But is your central heating up to the challenge? You could be in for a miserable time if not, so why risk it? Choose one of these money-saving offers from British Gas, and you can stay snug and cosy all winter.

Interest-free credit*

- Put down a deposit of 20%
- Spread your repayments for up to 24 months
- Don't pay a penny in interest

Or buy now, pay in six months†

- Pay a 10% deposit
- Then pay the balance in six months, interest-free, or spread the cost over one to five years (APR 26%)

The example below is typical of hundreds of such travel advertisements to be found in magazines and newspaper supplements.

Read and discuss

1 Study the China travel advertisement opposite which shows a balanced use of copy and visuals.

2 Then compare it with the British Gas promotion on page 65 in terms of its design features and the ways in which visuals and copy work together. Pay particular attention to the following things:

  ▶ photographs (of different sizes)
  ▶ the variety of different styles of type
  ▶ tinted boxes
  ▶ bullet points
  ▶ colour
  ▶ occasional capitalization
  ▶ selected text in bold
  ▶ the product illustration.

3 How successful are each of these design features in both advertisements?

4 Is one more successful that the other
  ▶ in some areas?
  ▶ in all areas?

Write

Plan and sketch out a magazine advertisement for a touring holiday – you choose the destination. Use the China advertisement and any other similar advertisements you can find as examples of the ways in which copy and visuals can be imaginatively combined. For this activity, it will be enough to
  ▶ write headings and a brief outline of the body copy rather than working on the details of phrasing (which will be covered in later units)
  ▶ describe the type of visual and where it will appear on your advertisement.

Homework

1 Find an advertisement which, in your opinion, creatively combines copy and visuals.

2 Mount it on a larger piece of paper to create a margin on all sides and add notes to it in a similar way to the British Gas example on page 65.

3 Then write additional notes on the advertisement's effective use of copy, visuals and graphics, using what you have learned from the examples in this unit.

Grammar

Learning aims	▶ To understand some of the **grammatical forms** which are commonly found in the language of advertising.
Facts	▶ Advertising has developed its own ways of saying things. This style is so recognizable that it is usually easy to tell when someone is reading out an advertisement, rather than a newspaper article or a letter.
	▶ The grammar of advertising copy can be quite distinctive as the examples in this unit show.
	▶ Compared with most other forms of prose writing, advertising language tends to:
	▶ use more **imperatives**
	▶ include sentence forms common in **spoken English**
	▶ follow different rules for **paragraphs**.

These extracts from advertisements for Hawkshead boots (below) and Daihatsu cars (opposite) show the use of the imperative, sentence forms common in spoken English and unconventional paragraphing.

Hawkshead Kids Boots. They're yours for pocket money.

Actually the second half of the previous sentence.

New paragraphs are used for every sentence (including sentences which are actually part of the previous sentence)

At Hawkshead we understand how expensive kids can be.

Especially when it comes to buying them decent footwear.

Which is why we developed these boots.

Priced at only £10, they'll take just about any punishment kids can give them.

Of course, running, jumping and tearing around can put a lot of stress on young growing bones and ligaments.

So we made sure the contoured insole was anatomically designed to cradle the foot.

There's also plenty of padding around the ankle and tongue, for extra comfort and support.

And you'll be pleased to hear the soft suede/Cordura™ fabric is as difficult to scuff, as it is easy to clean.

Our boots come in a range of colours and sizes. For a price that won't break the piggy bank. £10.

Guess how much. Guess again.

As £13,000 cars go, the Daihatsu Terios is something of a bargain. It has the manoeuvrability and convenience of a small car, but with the commanding driving position and reassurance of 4 wheel drive. Plus it has all the bits and bobs you'd expect for this kind of money: side impact bars and driver's airbag, power steering, central locking. The list goes on and on. And in the unlikely event that it should be off road for the wrong reasons there's a 3 year unlimited mileage warranty. The thing is it doesn't cost £13,000. It costs £9,995. Or better still, £99 a month at 10.81% APR* if you choose to finance it. For details call 0800 618 618. **The Daihatsu Terios. From only £9,995 on the road.**

DAIHATSU

◇ **CLEVER CARS FROM JAPAN.**

Car featured Terios+ £11,995. Price correct at time of going to press and includes VAT, delivery, number plates, 12 months road fund licence & £25 first registration fee. *Terios finance example: £3,900 deposit followed by 36 monthly payments of £99 and an optional final payment of £4,060. Total amount payable £11,609. 10.81% APR. Agreed contract mileage 6,000 miles per annum. £85 credit acceptance fee payable with first monthly payment. Applicants for credit must be at least 18 and a UK resident (excl. Channel Islands and Isle of Man). Credit facilities provided, subject to status, by Inchcape Financial Services Ltd. NWS House, City Road, Chester CH88 3AN. Written quotations on request. APR varies depending on cost of vehicle, deposit, length of agreement and agreed contract mileage. Ref: RRT2710

Grammar notes

Imperatives

When we want to tell someone to do something, we use a form of the verb known as the imperative. It is quite common in speech, but not used very much in written English except in instructions on official forms. However, it is used often in advertising.

EXAMPLE: Relax in a Radox bath;
            Write your name in block capitals.
            Buy now while stocks last.

Sentence forms common in spoken English

By using sentence forms more commonly found in informal spoken language, advertisers help to establish a closeness between reader and writer.

For instance, advertising copy frequently includes the second halves of compound sentences beginning with 'And' or 'But'.

EXAMPLE: And you'll be pleased to hear the soft suede/ Cordura fabric is as difficult to scuff, as it is easy to clean.

Advertising copy also uses dependent clauses which would normally be attached to the previous clause or sentence. These often begin with a conjunction such as 'Because...' or a relative pronoun such as 'Which...'.

EXAMPLE: Which is why we developed these boots.

Phrases which would normally be attached to the previous clause or sentence are also widely used in advertising.

EXAMPLE: Again and again.

Paragraphs

In common with tabloid newspaper reporting, advertising copywriters will frequently use very short paragraphs. This often involves breaking the text down into paragraphs of one sentence or even one phrase.

Read and discuss

The slogans below all come from leaflets advertising places of interest. The use of imperatives is very common in this kind of advertisement.

Explore the Chilterns
Travel through time at Beaulieu
Visit the National Waterways Museum
Discover the beauty of Henry VIII's majestic palace

Expect a warm welcome at the home of natural history
Warwick Castle - Experience a thousand lifetimes
Savour the splendour of Longleat House

1 Identify the imperative verbs in the list above and discuss what impact they have.

2 Then make up some slogans using imperatives to advertise other places of interest. These could be real places, perhaps near where you live, or places you have made up.

Write

This advertisement for Christmas trees appeared complete as a 'reader offer' in the *Telegraph* magazine. Redraft this extract from the copy so that it includes examples of all the grammatical features that you have learned about in this unit - imperatives, sentence forms common in spoken English, and unconventional paragraphs.

Christmas trees delivered direct to your door. Exceptionally priced from only £29.95.

Make shopping for a Christmas tree this year easier than ever. Have a top quality, attractive tree delivered straight to your door without any worries or hassle. Our artificial trees look just like the real thing, and will arrive ready for you to decorate. The deep green 'Canadian Spruces' come in 5ft, 6ft and 7ft heights, and require simple home assembly. They have a stable base, and will look truly seasonal decked with your favourite baubles and lights. Incredibly realistic and exceptionally priced there's no better choice for Christmas value or traditional Christmas style.

5ft tree only £29.95, 6ft tree only £39.95, 7ft tree only £49.95

Prices include carriage – order today.

Homework

Imagine that the Advertising Standards Authority has received a letter complaining about the 'bad grammar' in many advertisements. Write their reply, quoting from examples of advertisements in this unit, or others that you can find at home, to show how the advertiser's use of language (sometimes labelled 'ungrammatical') can actually add to the impact of a piece of advertising copy.

Colloquial language

Learning aims	▶ To identify the ways in which advertisers use **colloquial** language and to understand why they do it.
Facts	▶ Advertising copywriters are advised to use the kind of language that their customers might use in everyday conversations.
	▶ Rather like tabloid journalists, advertising copywriters usually find it effective to use **colloquial** rather than **formal** language. (See Unit 9, Facts section page 41.)

1 *Direct address to the reader*

2 *Conversational opening to the sentence*

3 *Mild insult to fit people, designed to get on the side of the unfit reader*

4 *Use of the first person plural pronouns ('us', 'we') for friendliness and to convey the idea that 'we are all in this together'*

5 *Colloquial expressions often used by advertisers*

6 *Compound word hardly ever seen outside advertisements*

7 *Jokey ending*

The copy used in this advertisement for an exercise bike is extremely informal in tone, thanks to the vocabulary and expressions of everyday speech.

Don't waste your time going to the gym.

1 If you're looking to lose weight, tone up or look after your heart, the only answer is regular exercise and a calorie controlled diet. So is going to the gym the **2** answer? Only if you want to waste time travelling to and from it just to waste more time waiting to use the machines, then suffer **3** intimidating stares from the body beautiful brigade.

4 It's no wonder so many of us join a gym with good intentions, only to find that we go less and less. Wouldn't it be much more convenient if you could get the exercise you need to stay healthy in the convenience and privacy of your own home? With the new Fitcycle range from NordicTrack you can do just that. **5** If your memory of exercise cycles is of a wobbly, uncomfortable machine that is more use as a clothes horse, then we've got news for you. Things have changed. NordicTrack is a leader in home fitness products with over 4 million satisfied customers world-wide. Our products are built to exacting standards and offer quality features you'd normally expect to find on gym models.

The Fitcycle offers a choice of three models, all with magnetic resistance for motion so smooth and quiet you can listen to your hi-fi or even watch television as you burn off the calories. Two of the models give you programmable workouts to add variety your fitness routine; and all feature at-glance displays showing you how much you're benefiting from your exercise. With an affordable, quality machine li this in your home, going to the gym re will be a waste of time. Try the Fitcycle yourself on 30 days home trial. You've nothing to lose except your spare tyre

Read and discuss

The advertisement below for Superdisk is written in an exaggeratedly informal style. The advertisers have opted to use language and visual images that reflect the product's main selling points – its compatability and simplicity.

1 Study the Superdisk advertisement carefully and discuss how both the copy and the visual images present a friendly and informal picture. Pay particular attention to
  ▶ the language used in the copy
  ▶ the style of the print
  ▶ the type of visual and the message it conveys.

2 How well does the style of this advertisement fit the overall message about the product?

3 What target group is it aimed at?

74 **Write**

Using the NordicTrack advertisement on page 72 as a model, write a short piece of copy in a similar colloquial style advertising a product of your choice. Include some of the features highlighted by the handwritten notes on the NordicTrack copy.

Homework

1 Find an example of some advertising copy which is written in a formal style and redraft it in colloquial advertiser's English.

2 Then, write a paragraph to explain
  ▶ how the two styles are different
  ▶ what effect each style has on the reader
  ▶ which target group each version might be appropriate for.

Words and wordplay

Learning aims

▶ To identify some of the features of **advertising vocabulary** and to learn the ways in which it is used.

Facts

▶ Advertising copy tends to contain many more vivid and positive words than would be found in other forms of writing.
▶ The vocabulary is also often chosen to suggest that the product has certain qualities which make it even more attractive.
▶ **Wordplay** is a common feature, and is similar in its effect to eye-catching and amusing images.

Vivid, positive and unreserved vocabulary

The following cutting from a holiday advertisement shows examples of typical advertising vocabulary that you might be asked to comment on in the exam.

SEVEN MILES OF SERENITY

Sandals Negril is a couples-only paradise situated on Jamaica's famous 'Seven Mile Beach' ... miles of powder white sand that provide the backdrop for pleasure, relaxation and romance ... perfect for a holiday or honeymoon ... perfect for a man and woman in love. With a choice of elegant accommodation including unique suites with concierge service ... four gourmet restaurants ... Sandals Negril is a world of luxury at an all-inclusive price with meals and drinks ad lib ... You can enjoy windsurfing, water skiing and some of the best scuba diving in the Caribbean ... play squash ... tone up in the fitness centre ... or sip cocktails at our swim-up poolbar ... nothing, not even expert watersports instruction, costs a penny extra.

Vivid words – conjuring up strong images

Positive words – evoking happiness

Unreserved words – suggesting that this product cannot be beaten

Read and discuss

1 Discuss the meaning and effect of the following examples of vocabulary in the Sandals holiday advertisement:
elegant   **unique**   **concierge**   **gourmet**   **luxury**

2 What impression are the advertisers trying to create?

'Quality' vocabulary

Sometimes the advertiser will select words which imply certain qualities, such as luxury or class, in the hope that readers will associate the product with that quality. In these three extracts from the same travel company leaflet, a different quality is given to each of the three cities by the choice of vocabulary: Paris has a fascinating variety of attractions; Brugge is relaxing; and Cologne is historic.

Welcome to *Motts Travel* Super CityBreaks

PARIS
4 days from £105

Paris.. No matter the time of year, is known as 'The Magical City'. Join us this Winter and we will show you!!

Paris conjures up many images for many people and is often referred to as 'Europe's most fascinating city'.

Enjoy gastronomic delights in a bistro in the Latin Quarter or sip a glass of wine in a pavement café on the Champs Elysées. See the famous Mona Lisa in the Louvre, the beauty of Notre Dame, the nightlife of Pigalle and Montmartre, the panoramic views of this historic city from the Eiffel Tower and beautiful Sacre Coeur. Gently cruise down the Seine by Bateau Mouche, window-shop on the elegant Rue de Rivoli, sample the glamours of the renowned Moulin Rouge — Paris literally has something to suit all tastes.

BRUGGE
Venice of the North
4 days from £119

Brugge — often described as the 'Venice of the North' and untouched by the industrial revolution that ravaged other European cities in the last century. Brugge makes an ideal centre for a relaxing break.

With its lacework of narrow cobbled streets, gabled houses and tree lined canals, and together with the friendliness of the Flanders people, Brugge is one of Europe's most beautiful and relaxing cities.

COLOGNE
4 days from £139

Cologne is a city of charming contrasts. The twin towers of the DOM, the world's largest Gothic cathedral, still dominate the skyline as in mediaeval times. Ancient ruins dating back to 50AD stand as reminders that this was once part of the Roman Empire. Visit the Roman Germanic Museum with its precious glass collection; walk the cobbled streets of the Old Town and discover the charming old buildings from the Middle Ages.

Read and discuss

Pick out the vocabulary in the Motts Travel advertisement which conveys the particular quality of each of the three cities.

Shocking the reader

Because we have come to expect the language of advertisements to be positive and associated with pleasant experiences, it comes as a shock when an advertiser deliberately introduces harsh-sounding, off-putting words. But this can be very effective in getting across certain kinds of message.

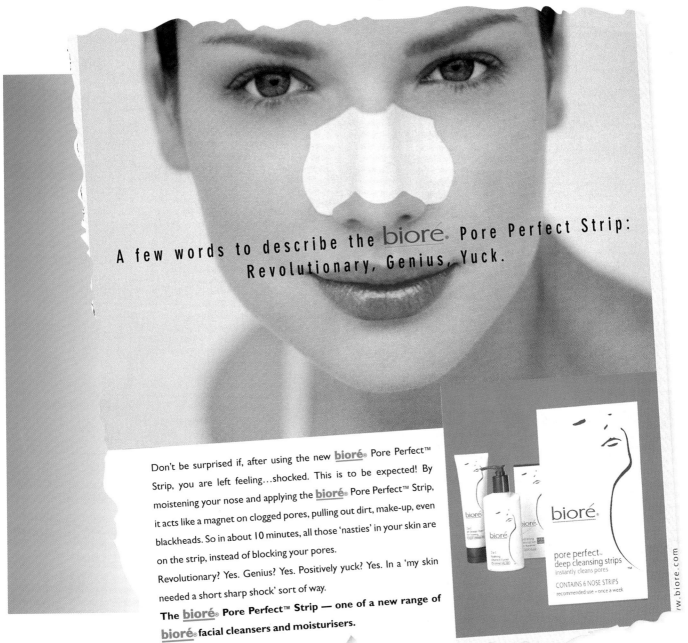

A few words to describe the **biore**. Pore Perfect Strip: Revolutionary, Genius, Yuck.

Don't be surprised if, after using the new **biore**® Pore Perfect™ Strip, you are left feeling...shocked. This is to be expected! By moistening your nose and applying the **biore**® Pore Perfect™ Strip, it acts like a magnet on clogged pores, pulling out dirt, make-up, even blackheads. So in about 10 minutes, all those 'nasties' in your skin are on the strip, instead of blocking your pores.

Revolutionary? Yes. Genius? Yes. Positively yuck? Yes. In a 'my skin needed a short sharp shock' sort of way.

The **biore**® Pore Perfect™ Strip — one of a new range of **biore**® facial cleansers and moisturisers.

biore®
pore perfect.
deep cleansing strips
instantly cleans pores

CONTAINS 6 NOSE STRIPS
recommended use – once a week

/w.biore.com

Read and discuss

1 Select the particular words and phrases in the Bioré advertisement which are deliberately off-putting.

2 Discuss why this might be an effective way of selling the product.

Wordplay

Puns are often used to attract the reader's attention, in much the same way as a witty image. Here are some examples of puns used to sell three different products: Cover Girl cosmetics, Nivea For Men moisturising lotion and Matki shower doors.

COVER GIRL

Spread the word. Not the Lipstick.

Introducing new Marathon Lipcolor
Check out our exciting new fade and transfer-resistant lipcolors. The Marathon range is kiss-resistant but with it's spectrum of vibrant colours, you certainly won't be.

COVER GIRL Niki Taylor
is wearing Marathon Lipcolor in Wildberry.
http://www.covergirl.com

heavenly showers

THE CONVERSATION MIGHT DRY UP BUT HIS SKIN WON'T.

NEW

MOISTURISING LOTION FROM NIVEA FOR MEN.
Of course, it takes more than great looking skin to get the girl. But it helps. New NIVEA For Men Moisturising Lotion protects your skin from the elements leaving it looking and feeling great. We could tell you why the Vitamin E and UV filters are so good, but trust us. You leave looking after your skin to us, and we'll leave the witty lines and sparkling repartee to you.

NIVEA FOR MEN WHO DARE TO CARE.

NIVEA FOR Men

FACE CARE
MOISTURISING LOTION
FOR NORMAL SKIN

FOR MORE INFORMATION CALL THE NIVEA Careline 0800 616977 (1 800 409576 REPUBLIC OF IRELAND)

Matki. With a gentle touch the smo... surround leaving a generous ope...

matki

...ange of shower doors and enclosures please t... ...8 or write to Matki plc, Freepost (BS7214), Yate, Bristol BS3...

Advertisements which appear in specialist publications, such as hobbies or sports magazines, often include puns related to the special interest. These three puns appeared in advertisements in a magazine published by the Royal Society for the Protection of Birds.

WATCH IN COMFORT. GET A GOOD HIDE.

SeeBirds
Guided Birdwatching Holidays in NE Scotland

Visit the great birding
east:

GET BITTERN

"The Lee Valley Park Bittern Watchpoint probably provides the best place in the whole world to see Bitterns in their natural surroundings" – Bill Oddie

What more of a recommendation do you need?

In recent years the reedbeds and plentiful food supply in the Lee Valley Regional Park have attracted between four and seven wintering Bitterns. They arrive from Europe and Scandinavia to escape harsh weather. But with these winter visitors there are probably less than 100 Bitterns in the whole country.

The Regional Park Authority is doing much to create more reedbeds, the Bittern's natural habitat. The Watchpoint, jointly managed with the RSPB, has been created to raise awareness of Bitterns and their need for conservation and to provide you with the opportunity to watch, enjoy and learn more about these secretive birds.

For further information on the Lee Valley Park Bittern Watchpoint, simply complete the coupon and return it using the FREEPOST address provided. Or, alternatively you can call the Lee Valley Park Information Centre on **01992 702222**

Lee Valley Park
Open spaces and sporting places

Please send me more information on the Valley Park Bittern Watchpoint:

Name ....
Address ....
.... Postcode ....
Tel. ....

☐ Please tick if you do not wish to added to our mailing list and sent fu information about Lee Valley Region

Please return to: Lee Valley Region FREEPOST, (ND 5193), PO Box 95 N17 3BR

Read and discuss

1 Explain each of the puns used above and on the opposite page.

2 Why is each one effective?

Write

Write a brief section of copy for an advertisement for a product of your choice, which makes use of at least two of the following:
▶ vocabulary used to create a sense of luxury, 'class', or romance
▶ puns
▶ deliberately off-putting vocabulary.

Homework

Choose a specialist publication and find examples of advertisements which use puns similar to the examples from the RSPB magazine above.

Sound-patterning

Learning aims	▶ To identify and understand the effectiveness of **sound-patterning** in advertising.

Facts

▶ To attract attention and be memorable, the language of advertisements will often use effects commonly associated with poetry. These include:

   ▶ **alliteration**: where a number of words in a sentence or phrase begin with the same sound or letter; for example: 'Chef's square-shaped soups show how good soup should be' (packet soup)

   ▶ **assonance**: a repetition of vowel sounds; for example: 'We knew how before you-know-who' (tonic water)

   ▶ **onomatopoeia**: when the sounds of the words help to convey their meaning; for example 'Mint-choc, mint-choc, mint-choc' echoes the tick of a clock (After Eight mints)

   ▶ **rhyme**: as in 'Let the train take the strain' (British Rail).

Read and discuss

Advertising slogans make good use of sound-patterning effects. These catchy little phrases which sound rather like proverbs are often repeated and are designed to stick in the memory.

Discuss which sound-patterns have been used in the following slogans (some of them from many years ago), and consider how effective they are in advertising the product.

A Mars a day helps you work, rest and play

BP — Britain at its best (petrol)

YOU CAN BE SURE OF SHELL

TWA — Leading the way to the USA (airline)

We're with the Woolwich (building society)

Electricity — clean simplicity

Guinness is good for you

DRINKA PINTA MILKA DAY

Great Little Rooster Booster
(eggs)

You'll wonder where the yellow went,when you brush your teeth with Pepsodent
(toothpaste)

Nice Cold, Ice Cold Milk

BEANZ MEANZ HEINZ

THE FREEZER-PLEEZERS
(frozen foods)

Put a tiger in your tank
(petrol)

When you need aspirin, drink Disprin

Electrolux brings luxury to life
(fridges)

Switch on the Sunshine
(breakfast cereal)

Write

Occasionally the choice of vocabulary in advertising copy succeeds in creating an onomatopoeic effect. Shampoos, for example, will frequently leave hair 'smooth, soft and silky...'

Devise some onomatopoeic phrases suitable for
▶ a hand cream
▶ a sports car
▶ a chocolate bar.

Homework

1 Do some research into advertising slogans and collect a variety of examples.

2 Then write an entry for an encyclopedia on 'Slogans in advertising'. In describing the word and sound-patterns they use, refer to the examples from your own research and those listed on the pages of this unit.

3 Finish off your article by selecting your three or four favourite slogans and explaining why you think they are particularly effective in helping to sell their product.

Persuasion

Learning aims	▶ To understand some of the **psychological** techniques used by advertisers to **persuade** people.
Facts	▶ In addition to all the features covered so far, advertisers have further selling techniques which involve making an appeal to our **emotions**.

There are many human emotions which advertisers can exploit in attempting to sell their products. Three of these are: our desire to be individualistic, our fears and our sympathies.

Individualism

An appeal to our individualism is frequently used in fashion advertisements, where the manufacturer wants us to change from an old product to a new one. The following examples of advertising copy are from Avon cosmetics, Dr Marten's footwear and La Redoute, mail-order fashion. They all follow essentially the same approach; they are saying to the reader: 'Prove that you're not like everybody else; show that you are an individual, not simply one of the crowd'.

Dare to **change** your mind about **AVON**

expect the Unexpected

Dr. AirWair Martens **with BOUNCING SOLES**
made like no other shoe on earth

There's no need to analyse individualism. Style is something which comes from inside, it's the way you are, the way you express it, the way you live it.

People want to be different. They want to be original, so take in the latest range of Dr. Martens ladies footwear at your local stockists.

LA REDOUTE

Don't run with the pack

Stand out from the crowd with the latest French fashions

Fear

Parents' anxieties for their children can also be a useful advertising tool, as this example shows.

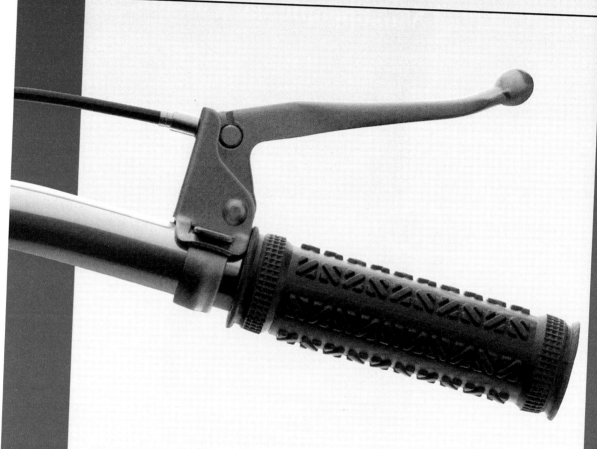

To appreciate Halfords adjustable brake levers, put your child's hand on this page.

This is the hand grip and brake lever of a child's bike, shown actual size.

According to the retailers, the bike is suitable for children as young as 4 years old.

The retailers, we hasten to add, are not Halfords.

Because all Halfords children's bikes are fitted with adjustable brake levers.

By turning a simple screw, you can adjust the reach of the brake levers to suit your child's hands.

As our picture demonstrates, not all children's bikes are made this way.

Which means not all children will be able to reach the brakes.

And if there's one thing more important than learning how to ride a bike, it's learning how to stop one.

HALFORDS WE GO THE EXTRA MILE.

Sympathy

Charities and campaigns have different aims from commercial companies, in that they are not selling a product in its narrow sense. However, they still want our money or our support, and understandably devise their advertisements in such a way as to make an appeal to our human sympathy, as this example shows.

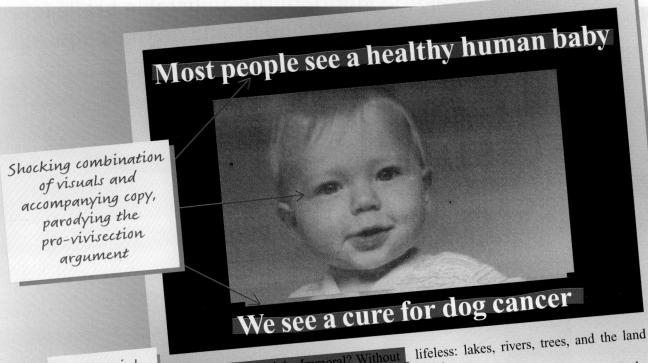

Most people see a healthy human baby

We see a cure for dog cancer

Shocking combination of visuals and accompanying copy, parodying the pro-vivisection argument

Colloquial 'question and answer' technique

Use of statistics

The excessive, unreserved language of advertising

Outrageous? Certainly. Immoral? Without doubt. Scientifically nonsensical? Of course – but no more so than the million-billion 'medical research' empire asking us to believe that it is possible to find cures for human diseases by experimenting on healthy animals.

In the US, prescription drugs are the fourth biggest killer, killing more than 100,000 people every year, and damaging millions of others.* One in seven births involves a deformity. Although the drugs industry and British government cannot, or will not, disclose figures, there is little doubt that we have a similar situation here.

Still the plague of chronic, degenerative and medically-induced diseases spins further out of control. Research in to cancer, heart disease, diabetes, arthritis, asthma, etc., etc., has been a colossally expensive, total failure. Meanwhile, environmental damage from millions of 'animal safety-tested' synthetic chemicals has rendered many areas of the planet lifeless: lakes, rivers, trees, and the land itself.

This lunacy is costing us plenty, with the vivisection-based NHS now swallowing some forty billion pounds each year. The reason for this dismal state of affairs is simple: the laboratory animal is a worse than useless tool in both medical research and human safety testing. If you are one of the millions who have suffered bereavement, or who are seriously ill because of fraudulent research, remember that if it is 'safety-tested' on animals, human are the REAL Guinea-pigs. Before you take any more drugs, or allow your child to be vaccinated, find out the facts. The BAVA is a voluntary organisation dedicated to the promotion of honesty in medicine and research. The opposition is extremely powerful and controls most of the media. We hope that you share our concerns.

*Journal of the American Medical Association, April 1998.

HELP US IN OUR FIGHT AGAINST MEDICAL FRAUD

British Anti-vivisection Association
PO Box 82, Kingswood, Bristol BS15 1YF

http://www.eurosolve.com/charity/bava

Read and discuss

What kind of impact does the British Anti-vivisection Association advertisement opposite have on the reader? The questions below may help you to get started.

▶ What do both the visual and the copy make you feel?
▶ How do they do this?
▶ How does the advertiser want you to react?
▶ Is it a successful advertisement?

Write

Write a review of the Halford's brake levers advertisement on page 83. Try to show how effective you think it is by referring to the following:

▶ the combination of visuals and copy
▶ the design features
▶ the use of unconventional grammar
▶ any other features covered in Units 11-20.

Homework

1 Look at the advertisement on page 86 for World Vision and compare it with the one promoting the British Anti-vivisection Association on page 84. Then try to answer the following questions:

▶ How effective is the combination of visuals and copy?
▶ Which register (colloquial or formal) has been used and how successful has this been?
▶ How effective is the use of statistics?
▶ Is the language used unrestrained or restrained and does it work in this advertisement?
▶ Are there any other relevant points that you could make?

2 Now give your opinion on which of the two advertisements – British Anti-vivisection Association or World Vision – you consider more effective.

Alem's life chances...

These are the life chances of Alem and other children like her in Ethiopia:

Alem's life chances...

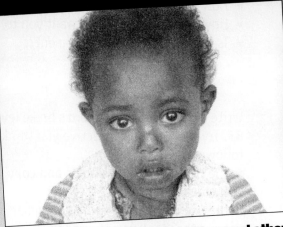

These are the life chances of Alem and other children like her in Ethiopia:

Living until the age of five:	82%
Receiving proper healthcare:	46%
Having clean water to drink:	25%
Being able to go to school:	19%

At World Vision, we believe these odds are simply unacceptable. You can help us improve them.

Sponsor a child like Alem, and you'll enable us to bring about real and lasting change through vital development work in her community, making it a healthier, happier place to grow up in.

Please give a child a better chance in life.

For a Child Sponsorship information pack, call

0800 50 10 10

or return the coupon to

World Vision, FREEPOST MK1730, Milton Keynes, MK9 3YZ

Please send me a Child Sponsorship information pack.

Title ____ First name _____ Surname _____

Address _____

Postcode _____ Telephone _____ MC9902

Return to:
World Vision
FREEPOST MK1730
Milton Keynes MK9 3YZ
Registered Charity No. 285908

World Vision

Introduction

Most GCSE English examinations feature a paper which asks you to answer questions on printed media materials. Sometimes this will be called a 'Media' paper; sometimes it will be titled 'Non-fiction and Media' or just 'Non-fiction'. But the skills you are asked to demonstrate will be the same.

Usually, your Media paper will be an 'unseen' examination. That means that you will be asked questions on passages which you have not previously studied. To prepare for it, you will probably work in class and at home on a range of newspaper articles, advertisements, leaflets, brochures, and mail-shots. All of this practice will help you to build up a range of strategies to tackle whatever texts you may encounter in the exam.

This book has been written to help students preparing for the Edexcel Media papers, but it will also help you if you are preparing for other unseen exams in English.

Getting started

What's in the paper?

The Edexcel Media paper is a two-hour exam. It consists of one or more pieces of 'text' – which could be a newspaper article or report, an advertisement or an information leaflet – followed by three questions.

Question 1 is the reading question. Your aim here is to show the examiner that you understand the question and that you can answer it accurately using appropriate examples from the text to highlight the points you make.

Questions 2 and **3** are the writing questions. These require you to write in a particular style and for a specific audience. Therefore, it is important that you choose an appropriate writing style for the task you have been set. If the question asks you to write a formal piece such as a letter to a newspaper, and you use casual, informal language of the sort that you might use in a conversation with close friends, you will not be judged to be writing appropriately and you will lose marks.

See Section 3, pages 109-127 for details of the Main Assessment Objective and Supporting Assessment Objectives for Questions 1, 2 and 3.

For both writing questions, you may need to refer to points you made in your answer to Question 1 and/or to specific details from the text. You may also be asked to write on a theme related to the subject matter of the text and bring in your own experiences and opinions to support your answer.

Using the exam time well

Within the two hours you are given to do this exam, you must give yourself time to read the paper in full to get an overview and then allow yourself a set amount of time for the reading, planning and writing required for each question. It is always wise to leave a bit of time at the end of the exam to check through your paper for mistakes. Below is a suggested timetable of how you might spend the two hours you are given to do the exam.

Minutes	Advice
0-10	Don't be tempted to launch into writing your first answer within the first 10 minutes. Give yourself time to read the text(s) to get an overview. Look at all three questions so that you are clear about what you will need to do in order to complete the paper.
11-20	Re-read the text(s) closely to prepare yourself for answering **Question 1** – the reading question. Use highlighter pens or underlining to identify key points which you will use in your answer. Organize your answer into paragraphs, and make sure that all of the bullet points in the question are addressed.

Minutes	Advice
21-50	Write your answer to **Question 1**.
51-55	Re-read **Question 2** – the first writing question. Plan your answer.
56-80	Write your answer to **Question 2**.
81-85	Re-read **Question 3** – the second writing question. Plan your answer.
86-110	Write your answer to **Question 3**.
111-120	Check through all three answers – carefully. There won't be time for major changes but you should correct spelling and punctuation errors, as well as any slips of the pen that you notice.

Are spelling and punctuation important?

Correct spelling is an important aspect of any piece of written work you do. However, **Question 1** is testing your **reading skills** and you will not lose marks because of the odd spelling mistake or misplaced comma. It is, however, important to express your ideas as accurately as possible so that your meanings are conveyed clearly. If your writing is muddled and confusing, you will not be giving the examiner evidence that you understand everything thoroughly. Some candidates in past years have lost marks **not** because they fail to understand the passage and the question, but because they don't communicate that understanding effectively.

In **Questions 2** and **3** you are assessed on your **writing skills**. You need to express your ideas clearly and accurately, but it is also important to remember that this time the examiner will be looking closely at your spelling, punctuation and other aspects of technical accuracy too. Spelling errors and faulty punctuation certainly will affect your mark on these questions.

The text

This text and the following three questions were used in the June 1997 Foundation Tier paper. Candidates were asked to study this advertisement for the Sinclair ZETA, an electric motor designed to be attached to bicycles.

TAKE THE SLOG OUT OF CYCLING

THE NEW SINCLAIR ZETA TRANSFORMS YOUR BIKE FROM PEDAL POWER TO ELECTRIC POWER IN MINUTES TO GIVE YOU EFFORTLESS CYCLING. JUST £144.95 DELIVERED.

Have you ever cycled up a hill and had to get off and walk? Or cycled into a stiff breeze, getting nowhere fast?

Have you ever wished someone would come up with an ingenious invention to take the effort out of pedalling when it gets too much?

The device you've been waiting for has just been invented.

Called The Sinclair ZETA, it's a world's first. The inventor is none other than Sir Clive Sinclair, originator of the pocket calculator. Like most brilliant

MAINTENANCE FREE

inventions, ZETA is simplicity itself. A neat, electric power unit transforms your bike from pedal power to electric power, greatly reducing the amount of effort needed to pedal.

To use ZETA, simply touch the "on/off" switch on the handlebar.

ZETA is so well engineered that it's maintenance free and works well in all weathers. What's more, you can fit it to your existing bike in a matter

SIMPLE 'ON'/'OFF' CONTROL

MAXIMUM SPEED: 14 mph.
RANGE: 10 - 30 MILES.
NO TAX, INSURANCE OR LICENCE REQUIRED.

ZETA

SIMPLE BATTERY RECHARGE

of minutes.

The battery pack and charger are included in the price, and the battery can be fully recharged for less than 1p.

SAFE IN ANY WEATHER

Charging can be carried out in situ, or by removing the battery from the unit. You can also purchase a back-up battery to carry with you to extend your range.

LESS THAN 1p FOR A RECHARGE

Depending on how much use it gets, the battery could last up to as long as 5 years.

The distance you can travel on one battery will vary depending on how much effort you put in. By reserving ZETA for gradients and headwinds, you could get up to 30 miles. If you don't pedal at all and let ZETA do all the work for you, then you can expect to get about 10 miles.

ENVIRONMENTALLY FRIENDLY

The beauty of ZETA is that it will go wherever your bike goes, making it ideal for relaxed cycling with the family at weekends, or going to and from work without effort. And, just like your bicycle, ZETA requires no licence, tax or insurance. It has a top speed of 14 mph and can be legally ridden by anyone over the age of 14.

Priced at just £144.95

SINCLAIR ZETA

Send to: VECTOR SERVICES LTD., 13 DENINGTON ROAD, WELLINGBOROUGH, NORTHANTS NN8 2RL. TEL: 0933 279300.

SINCLAIR RESEARCH LTD., 15-16 MARGARET STREET, LONDON WIN 7LE

GRADIENTS DISAPPEAR: HEADWINDS VANISH. CYCLING BECOMES ENJOYABLE AGAIN.

including VAT and delivery, ZETA is not available in the shops. So, fill in the coupon at the bottom of the page, or telephone your order on 0933 279 300.

Each ZETA unit carries an unconditional one year guarantee; and your money will be refunded in full if not totally satisfied.

✂ -

Send to: VECTOR SERVICES LTD., 13 DENINGTON ROAD, WELLINGBOROUGH, NORTHANTS NN8 2RL. TEL: 0933 279300.

Please send me:
Sinclair ZETA .... (Qty) @ £144.95 each.
back up batteries .... (Qty) @ £29.95 each.
　　　　　　　　　Total order value: £ ....
Packing and Postage included (UK and Channel Islands orders only).
Please allow up to 28 days for delivery.

☐ I enclose a cheque payable to Sinclair Research Ltd. for £ ....
Or debit my credit card: ☐ Visa　　☐ Mastercard

Expiry Date: Month .... Year ....
Card Number:

For telephone orders, call our Credit Card Hotline on 0933 279300.

MOPS
REG. NO. 8410

SIGNED ....
NAME ....
ADDRESS ....
....
TEL NO ....
Delivery address if different from above:
....
....

Answering question 1

Question 1 will assess you on your reading skills to see whether you can evaluate how the information is presented in this advertisement. Your first job is to read the question carefully.

QUESTION 1

(20 marks for Reading)

> In what ways does the advertisement try to persuade you that the Sinclair ZETA would be a good buy? Your answer should refer to:
> ▶ the information given
> ▶ the use of language
> ▶ the use of illustrations and graphics
> ▶ the overall design and layout of the leaflet.

How should I tackle this question?

One of the key words in this question is **persuade**. The examiner is looking mainly for evidence that you can evaluate this advertisement as a piece of **persuasive** writing. The question to ask yourself is: how does this advertisement turn me – the reader – into a customer who will want to buy the ZETA? The **four** bullet points make it clear that there are **four** aspects that need to be covered in your answer.

The next step is to re-read the advertisement closely and to make a note of the details from the text which you will refer to in your answer. Remember, you are looking for the persuasive features of this advertisement. What are they? You need to find examples of persuasive features for each of the four bullet point headings.

You will find it helpful to use coloured highlighter pens. Use a different colour to highlight evidence for each of the four bullet points. Don't be afraid to circle details or make notes on the advertisement too. This approach will also help you to organize your answer so that you deal with each bullet point in a separate paragraph. If you don't, your answer may seem disorganized and unclear.

You should spend approximately **10 minutes** on this reading and planning stage, and you should begin writing only after you have:
▶ studied the advertisement thoroughly
▶ selected the material you will use
▶ planned how to organize your answer.

You have about **30 minutes** to write your answer. As you write, keep asking yourself the question: Is this point relevant to the question? If it is not, then leave it out.

One mistake that some candidates made on Question 1 was to **describe** the ZETA advertisement in great detail instead of **explaining** and **analysing** its persuasive features – and that is the main point of the question. You need to **comment** on what your examples show about the persuasive features of the advertisement. It is not enough simply to say that a particular phrase is persuasive. It is also important to show **how** particular persuasive effects are achieved. You can do this by thinking about your own responses, and the possible responses of other readers, to particular aspects of the text – the language including the headlines, the content, the layout and design, etc.

A simple and effective three-part technique for doing this is to **describe**, **quote** and **comment**. This is how one candidate did it in answer to this question:

Describe	The advertisement starts off by asking questions to attract the attention of the target audience and to make them think about their own bikes:
Quote	"Have you ever cycled up a hill and had to get off and walk or cycled into a stiff breeze getting nowhere?"
Comment	So the advertisement first asks questions and then it goes on to give a solution. The way it does that is by talking about the problems of a normal bike and then switching to a positive view by showing how the ZETA overcomes these problems.

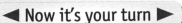 **◄ Now it's your turn ►**

1 Now it is time to have a go at Question 1. Allow yourself **10 minutes** reading and planning time and **30 minutes** writing time. Work on your own, and where possible under examination conditions. You may refer to the advice given above for tackling this question.

   Remember, you are not expected to say everything that could be said about the advertisement. What you should do is to select your best points and make these as effectively as you can in the short time you have to write your answer.

2 Now read the sample answer on pages 94-95. This is how one C-grade candidate tackled the question and how the examiner responded to what was written.

The advertisement uses many ways to make you think that the Sinclair ZETA is a good buy. Firstly, the heading of the advertisement would attract any cyclist: "Take the slog out of cycling", would certainly grab my interest. So the heading gets a reader's attention well, but then you read the sub-heading and it makes you even more keen to read the fairly lengthy advert. The sub-heading mentions that you could transform "Your bike from pedal power to electric power in minutes to give you effortless cycling". It then goes on to tell you of the price of 'only' £144.95 plus delivery. The price £144.95 seems to make the product seem cheaper than the rounded £145.00. I feel that if I was someone who used a bike a lot, I'd want to buy the Sinclair ZETA already!

The type of information given in the advert really does make the Sinclair ZETA seem like a great buy. It says it is a world first brilliant invention which takes the effort out of pedalling when it gets too much, so already you think that this product being offered to you is great. Throughout the advert they mention the words 'simple' and 'simplicity'. These words are mainly included in the text when talking of how to use the Sinclair ZETA, how it is fitted and how it can be put onto your existing bike. They say the 'ZETA is simplicity itself'. All of these kind of statements are intended to put to rest any worries you might have about this amazing invention being hard and complicated to use. They also tell you that it is maintenance free, works well in all weathers, makes cycling almost effortless in normally difficult situations, has a top speed of 14 mph and many more wonderful things about the ZETA. Other than this it gives you information on the battery, how long it lasts, how easy it is to change and more. The information given on the ZETA only adds more and more to its appeal. There is a

---

Annotations:

- Clear, direct opening
- A good quotatation to use but you need to explain exactly why it attracts your interest
- Good point to include but draw attention to the key word 'effortless'
- 'Great' is not a very precise word to use here. Can you think of a better choice?
- It's good to focus on key words like these, but better to comment more on the effect they are intended to have on the reader
- Don't use words like 'amazing' and 'wonderful' too often. You need to explain how the advertisement works, not show that you believe every word!
- These are well-chosen details which address the first bullet point of Question 1 (the information given)

Don't be too quick to accept the claims at face value – the most important question is: are these claims true?

This may be an accurate comment but you need to give some evidence – use brief quotations to back up what you say

This needs to be more precise: refer to details and explain why these illustrations are appropriate and how they might help to persuade the reader

This is too general – be more specific in your analysis

A good point

This is an abrupt ending: can you think of a brief closing comment to round off the answer?

lot of information given in the advert and this makes it almost impossible for you to need to ask any questions about it. This is useful because as it is only available to order it gives you no need to hold back on buying.

The use of language in the advert also helps to add to the appeal of the ZETA. The language used is simple and straightforward. There are no complicated words to think about. Also the questions asked at the very beginning of the advert such as "Have you ever cycled up a hill and had to get off and walk?" really make the ZETA seem like the perfect solution to all these problems.

The illustrations used in the advert are clear and well done. They provide a good look at what the ZETA will look like on your bike, which is important. The little pictures around the page with captions underneath like "Less than 1p for a recharge" or "safe in any weather" make you want to buy the ZETA even if you were only skimming over the page.

The layout and presentation of the advert is very attractive and clear. It attracts your eye straight to the advertisement if you were reading a magazine or newspaper and is very clear and simple to read.

Also the way ZETA is always written in capital letters really makes the name stick in your mind. This way you won't forget the product.

3 Now work in pairs. Swap your papers and, using the answer above and the examiner's comments as an example, go through your answers together circling the good points each of you has made.
▶ Have you missed anything out?
▶ Have you found things that the C-grade candidate missed?

4 Again, look at the examiner's comments. Is there any advice that you can give on how your partner's answer might be improved?

Answering question 2

Question 2 will assess your ability to use a particular form of writing – a letter, a report or an article – for a specific purpose. This might be a letter of complaint to a newspaper or a report written by a pupil for the school governors. You will need to show that you can **analyse**, **review**, and **comment** in your answer.

QUESTION 2
(20 marks for Writing)

> **Range of Writing: analyse, review, comment**
>
> A newspaper prints a story criticising the ZETA. Imagine you have used the ZETA. Write a letter to the newspaper giving your views.
>
> You should write about whether or not:
> - it is reliable
> - it is easy to control
> - its performance matches the claims in the advertisement
> - it is good value for money.

Preparing your answer

What you have already written in Question 1 will be helpful preparation for this writing task. The first thing to do now is to try to imagine what the newspaper article might have said about the ZETA. You know the article has been critical – for instance it might have said that the ZETA didn't work as well as the manufacturers claimed.

Look back at the advertisement for the ZETA on pages 90-91 to see what it was supposed to do. Then, note down the sort of things the newspaper story might have said about the ZETA. Your list might start like this:

> ○ It doesn't work well in bad weather.
> ○ I don't feel safe going down hill – worry I can't make it stop in an emergency.
> ○ The battery needs recharging too often.
> ○ It's too much hassle; it's easier and cheaper to manage without it.

Your notes will provide a good basis for writing a letter to the newspaper in which you give your opinions as a ZETA user. It is up to you whether you defend the ZETA or attack it.

Analyse, review, comment

It is not enough simply to describe in your letter what happened when you used the ZETA. Instead you need to draw on your experiences as a ZETA user to **judge** or **evaluate** its performance. To do this successfully, you must show that you can **analyse**, **review** and **comment** in your writing.

So, as well as describing your experiences, you need to:
- ▶ refer to evidence
- ▶ explain
- ▶ give reasons
- ▶ justify your comments
- ▶ draw conclusions.

This is how our C-grade candidate does some of these things:

Draw conclusions

> I found that in wet weather the ZETA doesn't work as well.

Justify your comment

> The drive from the motor isn't effective when it comes into contact with wet, muddy tyres.

Explain

> The problem is that the motor slips and the power is lost.

Finding the right style

Before you start to write your answer, make sure you have noted the key words in the question. You are asked to write a **letter** to a newspaper. This immediately signals a **formal** piece of writing and it is vital that your style is right for the task. Don't forget to think about format.

- ▶ How will you set out your letter – what do you need to include?
- ▶ How will you begin and end your letter?

The way you use language is very important in this question. You will need to express your ideas clearly and to organize them into effective paragraphs. Individual sentences must be straightforward and direct. Choose your vocabulary carefully. Make sure you say what you want to say precisely – vague expressions, poor punctuation and careless spelling can all weaken your answer. And remember, this is not a letter to a friend so chatty and informal language is not appropriate here.

You will need to make sure that you cover each of the **four** bullet points in the question. You must address all of these points to gain high marks. The bullet points are there to help you to organize and structure your writing. It is important to keep your answer relevant. The examiner will not be able to award high marks to responses that do not answer the question, no matter how well written they are.

◄ Now it's your turn ►

1 Now it's time to have a go at Question 2. Allow yourself **5 minutes** planning time and **25 minutes** writing time. Work on your own, and where possible under examination conditions. You may refer to the advice given on pages 96-97 for tackling this question.

2 Now read the sample answer below. This is what the same C-grade candidate wrote in response to Question 2 and how the examiner responded to the answer.

Dear Sir/Madam,

I am writing to you about the Sinclair ZETA. After reading the advert two months ago I decided that, as a person who uses bikes to get everywhere, the ZETA seemed like a brilliant buy. It would be an end to all of the problems they mentioned in the advert, but to my dismay it wasn't. As reliable as they said the ZETA was 'in all weathers', I'm afraid it just isn't. Although it has made some light relief of my efforts to pedal up a hill or ride into a stiff breeze, I've found that in wet weather the ZETA doesn't work as well. The drive from the motor isn't effective when it comes into contact with wet, muddy tyres. The problem is that the motor slips and the power is lost.

Added to this is the problem of controlling of the ZETA. It isn't as simple as the advert said it would be. It isn't as easy as touching an on/off button. This is because sometimes the 'on' button doesn't seem to work. Either this or the ZETA just doesn't work up to its expectations. Another thing that bothers me about the ZETA is how long the battery lasts. Yes, it is easy to charge, but once charged it

Be more precise in your opening sentence: 'I am writing in response to your recent article about the Sinclair ZETA'

'an advertisement for the ZETA'

The sense is clear although the expression is a little awkward

This explains the problem well

The control of the expression slips a little here – the explanation isn't completely clear

hardly seems to last long. I feel that with full-time use, even the 10 miles put in the advert (is a bit) (of) an exaggeration.

Although the ZETA isn't totally useless I feel that it is (no where) near the value for money I thought it would be when I ordered it. Unless all of the statements made about the ZETA in the advert were absolutely true, I don't feel that the ZETA is worth the £144.95 I (payed) for it. Considering the amount of work the ZETA does for me, which isn't much, I do not feel (totally) satisfied and will be asking for my money back. I think that your article which criticised the Sinclair ZETA was a fair one.

(Yours sincerely,)

A Bloggs

These words don't add anything so let's leave them out

One word – 'nowhere'

Correct spelling – 'paid'

'Totally' was used earlier in this paragraph – use 'completely' for some variety

Usually a letter beginning 'Dear Sir/Madam' would end 'Yours faithfully' but 'Yours sincerely' is acceptable in a letter to a newspaper

Correct spelling and layout. Well done!

Although the way you express your ideas is rather patchy – sometimes clear, but at other times awkward this letter is generally successful. The performance of the ZETA is evaluated and the letter communicates clearly.

3 Now work in pairs. Swap your papers and, using the sample answer above and the examiner's comments as an example, go through your answers together circling the good points each of you has made.
- ▶ Is your writing style appropriate to the question?
- ▶ Have you stuck to the point and kept your comments relevant to the question?
- ▶ Have you organized your answer well in careful paragraphs?
- ▶ Are your spelling and punctuation accurate? Have you copied words printed on the examination paper correctly?

4 Again, look at the examiner's comments. Is there any advice that you can give on how your partner's answer might be improved?

Answering question 3

Question 3 tests your ability to adapt your writing for a particular purpose or audience. You will need to show that you can **argue**, **persuade** and **instruct** in your answer.

QUESTION 3
(20 marks for Writing)

> **Range of Writing: argue, persuade, instruct**
>
> Write an article for a magazine for young people using this title:
>
> Cycling: the best form of transport for the 21st century?

Preparing your answer

A typical Question 3 could ask you to present **one** or **both** sides of an argument. You will be expected to write from your own experiences and include your own opinions. This can sometimes lead to surprises for the examiner, so it would be wrong for him or her to expect all candidates to cover the same points.

The question asks you to write an **article** for a magazine for young people. The key question to ask yourself is: Who am I writing this for? Your target audience is the young people who will read the magazine. Don't forget them. Their needs and interests will help you decide:

▶ what to write about in your article and
▶ how to write it.

What to write about

Look again at the question. The question mark after 'century' should signal the fact that you are free to argue **for** or **against** the idea that cycling is the best form of transport for the Twenty-first century. However, there are no bullet points to help you structure your answer. The planning is completely up to you, so making time to organize your answer is vital.

You could start by thinking about what issues are raised by the question. You might come up with the following:

o 'Best' form of transport for whom?

o 'Best' for what purposes?

o What about safety issues?

o What about environmental issues?

If you take the time and trouble to ask these questions before you begin writing your answer you will produce a much more successful article.

Now try to fill in some details for each of your bullet points. This has been started below:

BEST FOR WHOM?
Very young children?
Teenagers?
The frail and the elderly?
Fit, active and healthy people?
People who need to travel long distances quickly?
People living in towns with dedicated cycle tracks?
People who live in hilly areas?

BEST FOR WHAT PURPOSES?
People who need to carry shopping, goods, etc.?
People needing personal transport for short distances?
Business?
Leisure?

It would be difficult to argue that cycling is, in every sense and for every individual, the best form of transport for the Twenty-first century. It would be equally difficult to argue that cycling will become irrelevant in the Twenty-first century. If you argue a reasonable case in your response to this question, rather than taking up an extreme position, you are much more likely to produce effective and convincing arguments in your writing.

How to write it

As with Question 2, the way you use language is very important here. Remember, this is an article for a magazine for young people so choose your vocabulary carefully. You need to show that you can relate to the things that teenagers are interested in, but you still need to express your ideas clearly and organize them into effective paragraphs. Jumbled thoughts, unfinished arguments, poor punctuation, and careless spelling can all prevent your readers understanding your meaning.

Argue, persuade, instruct

When you get to Question 3 on the exam paper you will often have to decide whether it requires you to concentrate on building up a careful **argument** or to use **persuasion** to provoke the reader into a particular emotional response. Question 3 is much less likely to ask you to write to **instruct**; the main focus will be on **arguing** and/or **persuading**.

Argument involves **logical thought** and your writing should show that you can make a careful **assessment** of any **evidence** in order to arrive at a conclusion. For example, in this question you could **argue** that cycling is not the best form of transport for young children, the elderly and people who need to travel long distances.

Your evidence for young children might include:

- They may not have reliable balance skills and therefore may fall off a bike.
- They need careful supervision at all times by an adult.
- They would be in danger on most of our roads from cars or exhaust fumes.
- In bad weather they may get too cold and/or wet. Children are more at risk from hypothermia than adults.
- They may be too small to be capable of riding far.
- Bikes are expensive and children grow out of them quickly.

You could produce a similar list of points which would apply to the elderly and people who travel long distances to work. This would be the **evidence** which would help you form your conclusion.

If you were to take a more **persuasive** approach to the question you could also use **logical argument** to persuade your reader, but you may well use other tactics too. Persuasion often appeals to people's **emotions** – it speaks to their fears, worries, moral beliefs. It may also use flattery, appealing to their vanity – how they look and what they wear – or snobbery – where they like to be seen and who they like to be seen with!

Here are some of the issues you might raise when answering the question:

- Cycling is healthy – it keeps you fit not fat.
- Cycling is a growing, trendy sport – if you don't do it you won't be 'cool'.
- Cycling gear is fashionable – and you can buy lots of accessories.
- Cycling is something you do with your mates – if you haven't got a bike, you won't be one of the 'gang'.

You might also persuade your audience that other forms of transport are not trendy or convenient.

- Buses are dirty and smelly and don't always arrive when you want them to.
- Relying on your parents for lifts takes away your independence.
- Cycling is faster than walking.

◄ Now it's your turn ►

1 Now it is time to have a go at Question 3. Allow yourself **5 minutes** planning time and **25 minutes** writing time. Work on your own, and where possible under examination conditions. You may refer to the advice given on pages 100-101 for tackling this question.

2 Now read the sample answer below. This is what the same C-grade candidate wrote in response to Question 3. Again, the examiner has added comments on the answer's strengths and weaknesses.

Cycling: The best form of transport for the 21st Century?

We ask an important question: could bikes really be the transport of the millennium? Or should cars go on owning the road?

Think of it now. It's the year 2000, you're driving along, just like everyone else, in one of those big, futuristic beautiful cars that we all imagine. It's got those big rocket power engines coming out of the back and then...... Er, and then you wake up. Well that sort of thing is what dreams are made of after all, and we all know that technology isn't going to break all boundaries and bring us totally new and exciting, pulsating mega machines in time for New Year's Eve 1999. But even so, things could change. Nowadays wherever you go there are cars. I wonder how many people reading this article know the feeling of being stuck on a hot, stuffy bus or in a boiling car, and just sitting there waiting for the seemingly hundreds of cars in front of you to move on, even just a centimetre. Well, by the 21st century this problem will have got worse. The number of cars on the road is rising every year. If more people chose to use public transport it would help, but not everybody is willing to do this. But even this doesn't solve all our problems. There's still the big environmental factors. All cars and buses pump out huge amounts of waste gases every day. These gases are not only hazzardous to the

A good lively opening that seizes the reader's interest

A good place to begin a new paragraph

Language well chosen to appeal to young people

Another new paragraph

Good use of writer's (and readers') experience

Another new paragraph

Good word but only one 'z'

environment and the world around us but our health as well, such as to asthma sufferers.

But there is a form of transport that, if used more, could help the problem. (BIKES) Just think of how great they could be. No more traffic jams, no stuffy, packed buses. Just on your bike with the breeze lashing through your hair (oops, maybe not – always remember to wear a helmet.) Not only are bikes efficient they are also cheap to use and maintain. I mean bikes don't need petrol, insurance and parking fees. Hey, you don't even need a licence to ride one. Adding to the pluses of bikes is the fact that you'll be keeping fit and in tip top condition while using them. And just think all this while helping to save the environment. I definitely think bikes are THE transport for the 21st century. So hey, get into your garden and pull out that rusty old bike from the back of your shed. Blow off those cobwebs, fit it up, and get your dad to give it a lick of paint. Failing that show your parents this article and ask them nicely to please buy you a lovely new, top of the range, 15 geared, mountain bike.

The opening section explains the problem (traffic congestion, pollution) and now we turn to the solution – BIKES!

The title refers to 'cycling' but 'bikes' not 'cycles' is the word most young people would use

Good use of humour

Lively style

The tone and content are well judged to appeal to young readers

This answer raises key issues _and_ entertains the reader at the same time —enjoyable and successful writing.

3 Now work in pairs. Swap your papers and using the answer above and the examiner's comments as an example, go through your answers together. Circle the good points each of you has made.

▶ Is your style of writing appropriate to the question?
▶ Have you addressed your audience in an appropriate way?
▶ Have you structured your writing carefully and presented it in well thought out paragraphs?
▶ Have you stuck to the point and kept your comments relevant to the question?
▶ Are your spelling and punctuation accurate? Have you copied words printed on the examination paper correctly?

4 Again, look at the examiner's comments. Is there any advice that you can give on how your partner's answer might be improved?

Approaching a higher tier question

The examples of questions given so far have all been taken from a Foundation Tier paper. You may now feel that you would like to have a go at a Higher Tier question and read a sample answer.

Here is an example of Question 1 – the reading question.

QUESTION 1
(20 marks for Reading)

Read Boris Johnson's article from the *Daily Telegraph* – 'It's all Dastardly Nonsense'.

In what ways and how effectively does Boris Johnson attack Lady Howe's opinions about children's television?

You should comment on what Johnson writes **and** the way he writes it.

Boris Johnson is not impressed by claims that cartoons are rotting our children's brains

It's all dastardly nonsense

Poor Lady Howe is shocked. Kiddies' television is "dumming down", warns the chairman of the Broadcasting Standards Commission. The little brutes are watching even more cartoons, she has discovered, with airtime given over to animation rising from nine per cent in 1981 to 35 per cent in 1996.

Unless we have new regulations to restrict the broadcasting of cartoons, our nation's future will grow up soft in the head, she cries. Well, those of us whose brains were irreversibly corroded by watching children's television in the Seventies can tell her she is talking absolute bilge.

Ah, the pleasure, the relief, when the "improving" programmes ended, and some grown-up stopped hectoring you about making sink tidies out of washing-up bottles, and one of those Hanna-Barbera theme tunes would begin.

No jingle was more thrilling than *Hong Kong Phooey*. One minute he was a depressed-looking dog who worked as a janitor. Then, having changed in a filing

The adventures of Dick Dastardly and Muttley (left) and Penelope Pitstop (above) in *The Wacky Races* were welcome relief after earnestly 'improving' programmes.

cabinet into a black mask and dressing-gown, he was the planet's most fearsome exponent of the martial arts.

My colleagues and I regularly enact some of his routines. "*Nyah-Choi!*" we cry, before breaking into a chorus of "Hong Kong Phooey! Number One Super Guy! Hong Kong Phooey! Quicker than the human eye!" Then there was Top Cat, who lived a life of Horatian simplicity in his dustbin; when he was not thwarting Officer Dibble.

But these efforts, though fine, were eclipsed by two shows. I am thinking first of *Scooby Doo*, about the pusillanimous dog-detective. It has been

pointed out that *Scooby Doo* plots were always the same. Scooby, Shaggy and the gang would arrive at a motel or Coney Island amusement park to be met by a weeping owner/manager.

A ghost or werewolf was haunting the place and driving away custom, he would wail. Later, with magnificent narrative economy, the werewolf would be exposed as the fairground owner *himself*! It was all a cover to allow him to smuggle gold or nuclear weapons! Was this not a vital lesson for our young minds, about whingeing businessmen?

Finally, at the summit of the cartoonists' art, I would place *The Wacky Races*. What, Lady Howe, could be more illuminating of life? It was, and is, an endless, pointless struggle to be in the lead.

You may say that the characterisation was not deep. Penelope Pitstop, the Ant Hill Mob, the Hillbillies in the Arkansas Chugga-Bug; you could say they were ciphers. But let me ask: if Muttley always let down Dick Dastardly, as he did, if he always laughed his terrible laugh, why did Dastardly stick with Muttley? What bond kept them together?

I haven't the foggiest. But I tell you this, Lady Howe. The comedy of Dick Dastardly and his dog was worth any number of geezers in beards and sweaters telling us stories from wicker chairs.

◀ Now it's your turn ▶

You may find it helpful to re-read the advice given on pages 92-93 on tackling Question 1.

1 Allow yourself **10 minutes** reading and planning time and **30 minutes** writing time. Work on your own, and where possible under examination conditions.

Remember, you are not expected to say everything that could be said about the article. What you should do is to select your best points and make these as effectively as you can in the short time you have to write your answer.

2 Now read the sample answer below. This is how one A*candidate tackled the question and how the examiner responded to what was written.

> *Clear opening. Second sentence shows your overall grasp of the article*

Boris Johnson, using a variety of methods, attempts to attack Lady Howe's opinions about children's television. However, the article falls short of convincing the reader that cartoons are, as Johnson implies, a necessary part of children's television.

> *This is exactly the right word to use*

> *Well explained – a detailed commentary*

> *Precise, controlled expression*

One method employed by Johnson throughout the article is (ridicule.) In the opening lines he states: "Poor Lady Howe is shocked." This is effective since the word "poor" makes Lady Howe the object of amusement and suggests that she is prudish and easily upset. The effect of this is to encourage the reader to side with Johnson. Furthermore, Johnson's statement that "our nation's future will grow up soft in the head, she cries" causes Lady Howe's outrage to be viewed as ridiculous over-exaggeration of "the problem" of cartoons. This therefore contributes towards the ridiculing of Lady Howe and is effective in doing so.

The use of (irony) further serves the purpose of attacking Lady Howe and presenting her as foolish:

"those of us whose brains were irreversibly corroded by watching children's television in the Seventies can tell her she is talking absolute bilge".

The irony here is quite (amusing) because in the article as a whole Johnson really seems to be suggesting that it is Lady Howe's brain which must be soft if she is so worried by harmless children's cartoons. To say that someone is "talking absolute bilge" is very insulting and Johnson makes it clear that he has no respect at all for her views. By conveying his point in such an extreme way Johnson is being very persuasive towards the reader in undermining Lady Howe's opinions.

However, despite Johnson's success in attacking Lady Howe's opinions, his use of his own experiences is far less effective. He refers to specific cartoons like Hong Kong Phooey, Scooby Doo and The Wacky Races, and says:

"Ah, the pleasure, the relief, when the 'improving' programmes ended… and one of those Hanna—Barbera theme tunes would begin".

Although I haven't been deprived of television as a child, these cartoons are not ones I can remember, so Johnson seems to be appealing to an older generation which is able to share his experiences. Perhaps such readers would be convinced by Johnson's comments about these programmes but to the younger reader references to cartoons from several decades ago have little meaning and therefore fail to back up Johnson's objections to Lady Howe's opinions. To his credit though, Johnson does explain a little about the plot of Scooby Doo, then suggests a moral contained within the cartoon:

"Was this not a vital lesson for our young minds about whingeing businessmen?"

Although clearly not to be taken literally, the touch of humour here helps hold the attention of the reader while making a light-hearted objection to Lady Howe's criticism. Humour is also involved in Johnson's description of The Wacky Races:

"What, Lady Howe, could be more illuminating of life? It was, and is, an endless, pointless struggle to be in the lead."

The final paragraph of the article sums up Johnson's attack on Lady Howe's opinions about children's television:

Another precise word and a good example to quote

This is evidence of a genuinely _personal_ response to the article

Expression wavers a little here, but the sense is clear

A good use of your own experience as a basis for assessing the effectiveness of Johnson's reference to particular TV programmes

Comment and the quotation which backs it up are well combined here

Again, very effective use of quotation here

"The comedy of Dick Dastardly and his dog was worth any number of geezers in sweaters talking from wicker chairs". The point here seems to be that Lady Howe is linked with "geezers in sweaters–type children's television" — all very sensible and good for you, but so dull compared with the cartoons that children watch from choice.

In conclusion, Johnson's attack on Lady Howe's opinions about children's television is in some ways effective. His comments have the effect of turning Lady Howe into a figure of fun whose views no intelligent person could take seriously. Although I quite enjoyed some parts of the article, I have to admit though that Johnson didn't really seem interested in considering Howe's views in a careful and fair-minded way. The piece was entertaining but I couldn't say at the end of it that I'm convinced that Johnson is right about children's cartoons and Lady Howe is wrong. I'm sure that if you asked Lady Howe, she would say that Johnson didn't put her side of the argument at all fairly. I suppose Johnson's main aim was not to be fair but to be entertaining.

Intelligent thinking here about what the evidence in the report reveals about both Boris Johnson and Lady Howe

A very successful final paragraph – you have used points made earlier to arrive at a personal conclusion about both the arguments and the way in which the article was written

An excellent final comment

3 Now work in pairs. Swap your papers and, using the answer above and the examiner's comments as an example, go through your answers together. Circle the good points each of you has made.
   ► Have you missed anything out?
   ► What have you learnt from reading this answer and the examiner's comments?

4 Again, look at the examiner's comments. Is there any advice that you can give on how your partner's answer might be improved?

Finishing off

Ideally, you should leave enough time at the end of the exam to check through all your answers. The timescale on page 89 suggests **10 minutes**. You will only have time to check 'easy' details like missing full stops, obvious spelling mistakes (make sure you've spelt the key words used on the exam paper correctly!) and the odd 'scribbled' word which might be difficult for the examiner to read. It is well worth taking the trouble to make these final corrections. But remember they can never be a substitute for carefully planned, well-organized answers.

STOP MESSING WITH OUR NATURAL FOOD

Shoppers' anger at genetic crops

By TRACEY HARRISON and JEREMY ARMSTRONG

MILLIONS of shoppers opposed to genetic foods yesterday demanded: "Don't mess around with nature."

Green groups also called for urgent action after tests showed genetically modified potatoes can harm the immune system of rats and stunt their growth.

A poll yesterday found six out of 10 consumers are against genetically modified (GM) products.

But the Government last night refused to consider a ban on so-called "Frankenstein" foods, despite the new warnings.

Professor Arpad Puztai, of the Rowett Institute in Aberdeen, fed modified potatoes to rats for 100 days.

The potatoes had changes similar to those developed by commercial food producers to make crops resistant to pesticides.

Prof Puztai said his findings raised grave questions about the safety of genetic foods for humans.

Controls

He added: "We are assured this is absolutely safe and that no conceivable harm could come to

FRANKENSTEIN FOODS

Genetically modified ingredients are found in half our processed foods

breakfast cereal · bread · baked beans · ice-cream · crisps · margarine · chocolate

We're all just guinea pigs

GENETICALLY modified food is a "huge experiment with the human race as guinea pigs", pressure groups warned last night.

They claimed it is used in a wide variety of foods without proper research into the possible impact on human health.

In the US, genetically engineered cows were used to produce more milk until fears of a link to breast cancer.

A new wave of superbugs resistant to antibiotics is being linked to widespread manipulation of genes in food.

Friends of the Earth said a dietary supplement containing GM products was blamed for 37 deaths in the US.

Greenpeace genetics campaigner Jim Thomas claimed a small number of US pharmaceutical giants would soon "control world food – they are controlling seeds used, crops developed and even buying into food suppliers.

"They do their own tests and are not really looking for problems. There is not enough independent testing."

Dr Mae-Wan Ho, head of the Open University Bio-Electrodynamics laboratory in Milton Keynes, Bucks, said: "Safety regulations seem to have been relaxed. The public is being used against its will as guinea pigs."

us from eating it. But if you gave me the choice now, I wouldn't eat it."

GM ingredients are found in around half of our processed foods, including bread, baby food, margarine, chocolate and baked beans.

The supermarket chain Iceland has banned GM from its own label products.

Friends of the Earth and Greenpeace want GM foods taken off all supermarket shelves until more research has been carried out.

Friends of the Earth's Adrian Bebb said: "There should be more controls on imports and we would like supermarkets to follow Iceland's example and stop selling them.

"At the very least there should be proper labelling.

"At the moment people do not even know what they are buying."

Greenpeace's Jim Thomas said: "We are meddling with the delicate balances of nature."

But Foods Minister Jeff Rooker refused a ban in favour of "ultra-caution".

He stressed there were only four GM products on sale – tomato paste, vegetarian cheese, maize and soya.

Mr Rooker said the potatoes used in the tests would never have reached supermarket shelves.

He added: "We are not rushing with this science to get food on the shelves. We are taking a very cautious approach."

Under new regulations coming into force on September 1, all foods containing GM soya or maize must be clearly labelled.

But Tory health spokesman Alan Duncan said ministers should make a clear statement on policy to allay public concern. He said: "Massive forces are being unleashed.

"One of the basic human rights we need to re-emphasise is we should know what we are eating.

"There is clearly massive consumer suspicion."

Genetically modified food takes genes from one species and combines them with genes from another.

The *Mirror*, August 11, 1998

QUESTION 1
(20 marks for Reading)

Read the report, 'Stop Messing with our Natural Food', published in the *Mirror* on August 11, 1998.
In what ways does the report attempt to persuade the reader to oppose the use of genetically modified foods?

You should comment on:
► the language used, including any headlines
► the content, including opinions expressed by experts
► the overall design and layout
► any other aspects of the report which you think are relevant.

Main assessment objective

You need to show that you can:
► evaluate how information is presented.

Supporting assessment objectives

You also need to show that you can:
► read closely and carefully, referring to relevant details in texts
► respond to texts in a thoughtful and informed way
► follow an argument
► read between the lines to pick up what is hinted at as well as what is stated directly
► understand, describe and evaluate the various ways in which writers use language, structure and presentation to achieve particular effects.

QUESTION 2
(20 marks for Writing)

Range of writing: analyse, review, comment

Your school canteen manager has invited pupils to comment on school dinner arrangements so that improvements may be introduced next term. Write a letter to the manager offering constructive comments about present arrangements and improvements which you would like to see. You may comment on the menu, the seating arrangements and any other aspects which you consider relevant.

Main assessment objective

You need to show that you can:
► use a particular form of writing (a letter, a report, etc.) for a specific purpose.

Supporting assessment objectives

You also need to show that you can:
► communicate clearly
► organize your ideas into sentences and paragraphs
► use the grammatical structures of Standard English and a wide vocabulary to express what you want to say clearly and precisely.

QUESTION 3
(20 marks for Writing)

Range of writing: argue, persuade, instruct

The governors of your school are considering altering the school day by starting lessons at 7.30 a.m. and finishing at 1.30 p.m. School meals would no longer be available although snacks would be on sale during a 30-minute, mid-morning break.

All parents are to receive two leaflets, one arguing the case for the change and the other arguing the case to retain the present timings for the school day. Write a leaflet which presents **one** side of the argument. You should write the text only for the leaflet but you may, if you wish, include a simple diagram to show the format and design of the leaflet too. Do not produce illustrations or coloured headlines.

Main assessment objective

You need to show that you can:
► adapt your writing for a particular purpose and audience.

Supporting assessment objectives

You also need to show that you can:
► communicate clearly
► organize your ideas into sentences and paragraphs
► use the grammatical structures of Standard English and a wide vocabulary to express what you want to say clearly and precisely.

THE ONLY DAY OUT IN HISTORY THAT'S TRULY OUT OF THIS WORLD.

Both Madame Tussaud's and The London Planetarium offer excellent venues for a school visit. And now, with the help of our new education packs in Design & Technology, History and Science, you'll see your lessons – and your students – really come to life.

HISTORY

Madame Tussaud's offers you the unrivalled opportunity to bring your students face to face with the people who have made history. Introduce them to the likes of Elizabeth I, Sir Winston Churchill and Sir Francis Drake and bring the National Curriculum to life. Our new pack is designed primarily for Key Stage 2 and 3 and offers a wide range of imaginative topics, themes and time journeys covering Tudor and Victorian Britain, World War II and the French Revolution.

DESIGN & TECHNOLOGY

Madame Tussaud's traditional sculpting skills now combine with leading edge technology to produce audio animatronic figures.

Our new packs also offer a fascinating insight into the use of a range of materials from clay to sophisticated resins. Primarily for use at Key Stages 2 and 3, they provide an excellent resource which will add to your teaching in a practical, fun and interesting way.

SCIENCE

The London Planetarium adds a whole new dimension to the subject of 'Earth and Space'. School talks use the advanced technology of the Planetarium to complement the Astronomy component of the National Curriculum at Key Stages 1 to 4. And our education packs include teaching notes and activities which are designed to stimulate your pupils' interest in this fascinating subject. What's more, The London Planetarium can also be tailor-made to suit Special Needs groups. So bring your lessons to life. Bring your pupils to Madame Tussaud's and The London Planetarium in Baker Street, London.

MADAME TUSSAUD'S   **LONDON PLANETARIUM**

- -

Please send me more information concerning the Madame Tussaud's and London Planetarium Education Packs available, including details of special school rates.

Name _____   Position _____

School _____   Address _____

Postcode _____ Tel/Fax _____

Send this coupon to: Customer Services Centre, Madame Tussaud's, Marylebone Road, London NW1 5LR. Alternatively call our Customer Services Centre on 0171 487 0229.

QUESTION 1
(20 marks for Reading)

Study the advertisement for Madame Tussaud's and The London Planetarium.

In what ways is this advertisement aimed at an audience of teachers? You should focus on the language of the advertisement but you are also free to comment on the content and the overall design.

Main assessment objective

You need to show that you can:
► evaluate how information is presented.

Supporting assessment objectives

You also need to show that you can:
► read closely and carefully, referring to relevant details in texts
► respond to texts in a thoughtful and informed way
► follow an argument
► read between the lines to pick up what is hinted at as well as what is stated directly
► understand, describe and evaluate the various ways in which writers use language, structure and presentation to achieve particular effects.

QUESTION 2
(20 marks for Writing)

Range of writing: analyse, review, comment

Most primary and secondary schools organize visits and residential courses for their pupils. What do you think are the arguments **for** and **against** school visits and residential courses? Write a report for school governors in which you, a senior pupil at your school, present a balanced judgement on this topic.

Main assessment objective

You need to show that you can:
► use a particular form of writing (a letter, a report, etc.) for a specific purpose.

Supporting assessment objectives

You also need to show that you can:
► communicate clearly
► organize your ideas into sentences and paragraphs
► use the grammatical structures of Standard English and a wide vocabulary to express what you want to say clearly and precisely.

QUESTION 3
(20 marks for Writing)

Range of writing: argue, persuade, instruct

You have been given the opportunity to join an overseas tour next Easter arranged by a local club or organization of which you are a member. However, this would mean that you will need to miss the last week of the school term, and the club requires each pupil to write to the headteacher to ask for permission to take time off. Decide on the specific details of your tour – it could be a football tournament, a musical tour, charity relief work, an adventure trek or any other activity which you think might justify your request to the headteacher.

Write a letter to persuade your headteacher that your activity is worthwhile and that you deserve to be allowed to miss the last week of term.

Main assessment objective

You need to show that you can:
▶ adapt your writing for a particular purpose and audience.

Supporting assessment objectives

You also need to show that you can:
▶ communicate clearly
▶ organize your ideas into sentences and paragraphs
▶ use the grammatical structures of Standard English and a wide vocabulary to express what you want to say clearly and precisely.

OUTSTANDING VALUE AND AWARD WINNING SERVICE. SMILE, IT'S A SIMPLY PC.

Smile? I couldn't contain myself when I heard. Now Simply are giving away a free Iomega Zip drive with every 2010 PC!

Once I'd wiped the tears from my eyes, I phoned to check the offer was for real.

"It is," they said.

"Must be dodgy," I said.

"Far from it! In fact, Iomega are the market leaders in external Zip drives. This model stores a generous 100Mb of data and transfers it up to 20 times faster than a floppy drive. This model usually retails at £86…"

That confirmed my worst suspicions. Simply had lost it. I mean just take a look at the specifications of the 2010PC!

My advice to you? Call now before Simply regain their sanity on the 31st of October when the offer ends.

Quick, before everyone catches on!

UNBEATABLE PRICES

Outstanding value doesn't just apply to the 2010. Every Simply PC includes top quality components at really competitive prices.

The reason we can pass on greater savings to our customers is because of our buying power. As one of the UK's largest resellers you can be confident that Simply PCs include better performance at a better price.

GREAT SERVICE GUARANTEED

Our investment in customer service is winning us awards from major PC magazines.

For the second consecutive year we won service awards from PC Direct and Personal Computer World.

We swept the board in PC Direct Hits winning eight reseller awards, which included the all important one for *Customer Service Excellence*. And we won the approval of readers of PC World who voted Simply the *Best Hardware Dealer* of the year.

Our aim is to make every year an award winner. So if you're a first time buyer you can be confident we'll continue building on our good reputation.

FUTURE PROOF PCs

There has been a lot of publicity surrounding Year 2000 compliance. You can rest assured that Simply have taken this problem seriously. So seriously, that now we guarantee the hardware components that make up every new PC are Year 2000 compliant.

EASY ON-LINE ORDERING

All of the systems we feature have unique web addresses. So if you're interested in a specific PC, you can go directly to the relevant web page and buy it on-line.

Buying a PC on-line is safe and easy. Just enter your confidential credit card details and they'll be sent via a secure email direct to our sales team.

Once you've placed your order we'll aim to ship your PC in just seven working days and deliver it free. And remember when you order a PC on-line it entitles you to a free 32Mb RAM upgrade. So you'll get more performance with your new PC, courtesy of Simply.

BUILT TO ORDER

We know that our customers want the freedom to upgrade any PC. That's why this range is entirely flexible.

Our Simply sales team will provide informed advice about upgrading your system over the phone. Alternatively, if you feel confident about upgrading why not do it yourself at our web site?

Select any Simply system on-line and use our helpful pull down menus to customise the specification.

In one click you can change your processor speed or monitor size. As you alter the specification we'll add up the price on-screen, so you'll never pay more than you bargained for.

To take advantage of our unique on-line upgrade service visit our web site at: *www.simply.co.uk* or select the URL of any PC to upgrade the specifications.

PAYING FOR YOUR PC:

We accept Switch, Delta, Visa, Mastercard, AMEX and orders from the Public Sector and approved companies.

OUR SALES LINES ARE OPEN:

Mon - Fri: 8.00am to 8.00pm
Sat: 9.00am to 5.00pm

OUR CALL AND COLLECT SERVICE IS OPEN:

Mon - Fri: 9.00am to 8.00pm
Sat: 9.00am to 5.00pm
Sun: 10.00am to 4.00pm

SiMPLY COMPUTERS ™
FROM THE PEOPLE WHO LOVE PCs
0181 498 2118
2/3 Forest Works, Forest Road, Walthamstow, London E17 6JF

QUESTION 1
(20 marks for Reading)

The Simply Computers advertisement appeared in a specialist computer magazine, *PC Advisor*. In what ways is the advertisement directed at readers who have some knowledge about computers? How successfully do you think this advertisement achieves its aims?

You should comment on:
▶ the language used, including any headlines
▶ the content and organization
▶ the overall design and layout
▶ any other aspects of the advertisement which you think are relevant.

Main assessment objective

You need to show that you can:
▶ evaluate how information is presented.

Supporting assessment objectives

You also need to show that you can:
▶ read closely and carefully, referring to relevant details in texts
▶ respond to texts in a thoughtful and informed way
▶ follow an argument
▶ read between the lines to pick up what is hinted at as well as what is stated directly
▶ understand, describe and evaluate the various ways in which writers use language, structure and presentation to achieve particular effects.

QUESTION 2
(20 marks for Writing)

Range of writing: analyse, review, comment

What machines, devices or inventions do you think have had the greatest beneficial effect on the lives of members of your family during the last decade? Write the script for a radio talk in which you examine the benefits which have been brought about by either **one** or **two** of these things.

Your talk may be serious or humorous.

Main assessment objective

You need to show that you can:
▶ use a particular form of writing (a letter, a report, etc.) for a specific purpose.

Supporting assessment objectives

You also need to show that you can:
▶ communicate clearly
▶ organize your ideas into sentences and paragraphs
▶ use the grammatical structures of Standard English and a wide vocabulary to express what you want to say clearly and precisely.

QUESTION 3
(20 marks for Writing)

Range of writing: argue, persuade, instruct

'Traditional toys and games or state-of-the-art electronic gadgetry? Which should parents buy for their children?'

Write an article for a magazine for parents of school-age children in which you argue the case for **either** traditional **or** electronic toys and games. Use your own experiences and enthusiasms to persuade your readers.

Main assessment objective

You need to show that you can:
▶ adapt your writing for a particular purpose and audience.

Supporting assessment objectives

You also need to show that you can:
▶ communicate clearly
▶ organize your ideas into sentences and paragraphs
▶ use the grammatical structures of Standard English and a wide vocabulary to express what you want to say clearly and precisely.

The passive killer

By JENNY HOPE
Medical Correspondent

SCIENTISTS are calling for drastic curbs on smoking in public places after a report concluded that passive smoking does cause lung cancer.

The report from the Government-backed Scientific Committee on Tobacco and Health rejects claims by the tobacco industry at the weekend that no link could be proved between passive smoking and lung cancer.

As well as lung cancer, passive smoking can also cause heart disease and poses a special threat to babies and children, it says.

Babies whose parents smoke are twice as likely to be victims of sudden infant death and have a 50 per cent increased risk of suffering serious breathing difficulties. Asthma attacks, bronchitis, pneumonia and glue ear can all be triggered.

People who regularly breathe in others' smoke have an increased risk of lung cancer and heart disease.

Those living with a smoker have a 20 to 30 per cent increased risk of lung cancer and a 23 per cent increased risk of heart disease.

As for smokers themselves, half are killed by the habit unless they quit, the report says.

Smoking causes 120,000 deaths a year, accounting for a third of all cancer deaths and one in six other deaths. Among the health problems are lung, mouth and throat cancer, heart attacks, lung disease, cataracts, hip fractures and gum disease.

The report released yesterday on National No Smoking Day, is

Other people's cigarette smoke does cause cancer scientists confirm

expected to reinforce demands from anti-smoking campaigners for tough measures in a policy paper on smoking reduction due out later this year.

The scientists on the tobacco and health committee, led by Professor David Poswillo, have themselves produced uncom-

THE PRICE THEY PAY

FOR THE PASSIVE SMOKER

- Raises risk of lung cancer by 20-30%.
- Raises risk of heart disease by 23 per cent.
- Doubles the chances of a baby dying of sudden infant death syndrome when the mother smokes.
- Increases baby's risk of respiratory illness by 50%.
- Gives school children a 50-60% increased chance of developing asthma.
- Raises risk of children having 'glue ear'

FOR THE SMOKER

- Causes 120,000 deaths a year
- Causes 30,000 lung cancer deaths each year
- Lifelong smokers have a 15 times greater risk of disease.
- Doubles the risk of dying before 65.
- Raises risk of a range of cancers.
- Raises risk of heart attacks.
- Raises risk of cataracts.
- Raises risk of hip fractures through bone thinning.
- Smoking in pregnancy raises risk of miscarriage and low birth weight.

FAMILY CUT OFF FROM THE FUN

SOCIAL activities for Bob and Heather Conder's family revolve around other people's smoking habits.

Their two sons Keith, 13, and Clive, 11, have asthma and their breathing problems are triggered by exposure to cigarette smoke.

'As a family we can't go to places where they might be affected although it's a bit hard on our 12-year-old daughter Sarah who doesn't have asthma,' said Mr Conder, 43, who works for BT near his home outside Exeter, Devon. 'There are pubs, clubs and restaurants we'd like to visit together but we can't take the risk.

'Keith's medication has been changed to try to improve his condition and it seems to work.

'But our social activities are limited by smokers – their behaviour affects our behaviour. At wedding receptions, for example, when smokers move in we have to move out and sit in corners, looking anti-social.

'Even at the squash club we all belong to there can be a problem with people lighting up.

'A ban on smoking in public places is long overdue.'

promising recommendations, with the starting point that the 'enormous damage to health and life arising from smoking should no longer be accepted'.

'Public have to be protected'

They say: 'There is an importance and urgency with the smoking problem that needs to be recognised by both the Government and the public.'

Restrictions on smoking in public places are needed to protect public health and it should not be allowed in public service buildings and on public transport, other than in designated areas, the report says.

Wherever possible, it should be banned in the workplace.

It says the Government should make the tobacco industry accept smoking is a major cause of premature death and there should be better disclosure of the hazards to consumers.

Awareness of the risks of smoking in the home, especially to children, should also be increased.

It recommends raising the real price of tobacco each year to discourage smoking, especially by young people, and banning all tobacco advertising, promotion and sponsorship.

And it says nicotine replacement therapy should be more widely available, possibly through NHS prescription.

Anti-smoking campaigners said the report scuppered claims by tobacco firms that a World Health Organisation report had found no extra lung cancer risk for passive smokers.

The WHO has already accused the tobacco industry of staging a publicity stunt which was 'wholly misleading' about the conclusion of its study that a link does exist.

Chief Medical Officer Sir Kenneth Calman said the Government accepted the report and hinted its recommendations might be adopted in the forthcoming policy paper.

Dr Sandy Macara, chairman of the British Medical Association, said the tobacco industry should 'hang its corporate head in shame', adding: 'Its desperate attempts to escape responsibility have been trounced.'

But John Carlisle of the Tobacco Manufacturers' Association said the report's conclusions on environmental tobacco smoke were weak and inconclusive and did not justify further curbs in public places.

The *Daily Mail*,
Thursday, March 12, 1998

QUESTION 1
(20 marks for Reading)

Read Jenny Hope's report 'The Passive Killer' which appeared in the *Daily Mail*. To what extent does Jenny Hope's report take sides in the debate about the dangers of smoking?

You should comment on:
► the language used, including any headlines
► the content and organization
► the overall design and layout
► any other aspects of the report which you think are relevant.

Main assessment objective

You need to show that you can:
► evaluate how information is presented.

Supporting assessment objectives

You also need to show that you can:
► read closely and carefully, referring to relevant details in texts
► respond to texts in a thoughtful and informed way
► follow an argument
► read between the lines to pick up what is hinted at as well as what is stated directly
► understand, describe and evaluate the various ways in which writers use language, structure and presentation to achieve particular effects.

QUESTION 2
(20 marks for Writing)

Range of writing: analyse, review, comment

In an article about smoking published in the *Daily Telegraph*, Emily Mortimer wrote: 'I don't think there is any subject people feel so free to pontificate on; and the sort of people who are irritated by smoking are fast becoming the sort of people I delight in irritating.'

Pontificate: to speak in a self-important or dogmatic way.

Write a letter to the *Daily Telegraph* in response to the above comment. In your letter, suggest ways in which the rights of smokers might be balanced against the rights of non-smokers.

Main assessment objective

You need to show that you can:
► use a particular form of writing (a letter, a report, etc.) for a specific purpose.

Supporting assessment objectives

You also need to show that you can:
► communicate clearly
► organize your ideas into sentences and paragraphs
► use the grammatical structures of Standard English and a wide vocabulary to express what you want to say clearly and precisely.

Higher tier

QUESTION 3
(20 marks for Writing)

Range of writing: argue, persuade, instruct

Are newspaper and television journalists justified if they reveal their personal feelings in their reporting or should they remain as neutral observers at all times?

Write the script for a television 'talkback' slot in which you are given three minutes to present your arguments on this topic.

Main assessment objective

You need to show that you can:
▶ adapt your writing for a particular purpose and audience.

Supporting assessment objectives

You also need to show that you can:
▶ communicate clearly
▶ organize your ideas into sentences and paragraphs
▶ use the grammatical structures of Standard English and a wide vocabulary to express what you want to say clearly and precisely.

As I fell into the icy sea my nightmare became reality

David Hempleman-Adams tells how disaster struck in a snowstorm

Day 25 Sunday March 29. No satellite readings received and no radio contact.

Day 26 Monday March 30 **Position:** 85°21'N; 75°52'W; Walked eight miles and floated 14 miles north. **Temp:** -32C (with windchill -63C). **Hours of light:** 17hr 14 min

We are caught in the Beaufort Gyral Stream, an area of huge elliptical currents that have carried us first a long way west, then seven miles north, across the 85th parallel at 3am.

Of course we were overjoyed to pass another significant milestone, even if it was while we were lying in our tents sheltering from the fiercest snowstorm we've encountered so far.

Shortly before midday, we'd had enough of waiting around, and set off into a complete white-out. It was terrifying; when the sky blends into the ground and visibility drops to six to 10 feet then you know any wrong step could be the end.

After almost eight hours of gingerly edging our way forward, I was amazed to discover we had covered 15 miles, of which I estimate we walked eight, and floated the rest on the currents.

The bad news is that we have moved a long way east, indicating that the current will soon turn and drag us south.

Day 27 Tuesday March 31 **Position:** 85° 13'N; 76°28'W; Walked approx.

North Pole
Diary

two miles north but floated back 10 miles. **Temp:** -25C (with windchill -43C). **Hours of light:** 17hr 22 min

Disaster. Probably the worst day I've had in 15 years of polar exploration. Worried that we had come to the end of the northward elliptical drift and were heading south, Rune (Gjeldnes) and I hesitantly crawled out of our maggots – our sleeping bags – and set off into a total white-out.

The going was slow. The swirling currents of the Arctic Ocean brought back ice ridges with a vengeance and there was a lot of open water, difficult to spot until the last moment.

Then, when we seemed to be making reasonable progress, I fell through the ice. In a fraction of a second the recurring nightmares that have haunted me since I fell through ice in 1984 became reality. I slipped into the Arctic Ocean up to my waist, while standing on a hanging cornice of snow. In the white-out I had not noticed that it was only inches thick.

As I fell, I ripped my ice-spikes from the breast pocket on my windproof jacket and dug the two titanium nails into the nearest piece of white ice I could spot. I shouted to Rune, who was some way ahead,

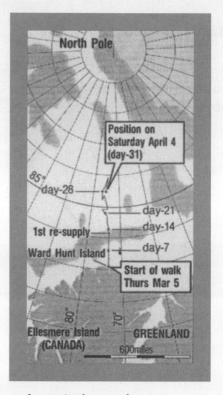

and seemingly out of range.

I lunged with all the strength I could muster for a blue piece of strong multi-year pack-ice two feet further ahead and dug an ice-spike in to the reassuringly solid surface. Then, as I was about to attempt another lunge, Rune emerged through the fog of the snow storm. He had stopped for a cigarette, and when I didn't catch up with him, had sped back to find me.

He dragged me on to an ice floe, where I lay, gasping for breath, my trouser legs already freezing solid like stovepipes.

Rune put the tent up double-quick, and lit the stove to warm it. Once inside, I stripped off my

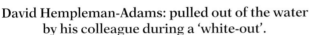

David Hempleman-Adams: pulled out of the water by his colleague during a 'white-out'.

sodden clothing and crawled into my maggot to inspect my legs and feet for signs of frostbite.

My clothes were frozen solid. With only one set of clothes, I will have to crack the ice off them each morning before I can put them back on.

To make matters worse, we floated south 10 miles, ending up further away from the Pole than this morning.

Day 28 Wednesday April 1 **Position:** 85°29'N; 76°40'W; Walked nine miles and floated seven miles north. **Temp:** -24C (with windchill -43C). **Hours of light:** 17hr 58min

The currents are on our side again, and we made good progress. Still a white-out, but no sign – yet – of frostbite.

Day 29 Thursday April 2 **Position:** 85°39'N; 75°33'W; Walked eight miles and floated two miles north. **Temp:** -34C (with windchill -65C). **Hours of light:** 18hr 32min

I am terrified of falling through the ice again, but we must plug on. We should be notching up higher daily mileages, but the snowstorm shows no sign of abating.

Although we have almost 24-hour sunshine, we haven't seen the sun directly for over a week and long for it to break through the fog of snow and ice.

Day 30 Friday April 3 **Position:** 85°50'N; 74°26'W; walked six miles and floated five miles north. **Temp:** -38C (with windchill -76C). **Hours of light:** 19hr 22 min

Extremely strong southerly winds are a mixed blessing; they push the ice northwards, but the windchill is crippling.

Day 31 Saturday April 4 **Position:** 85°29'N; 75°36'W; Walked five miles north and half a mile west. **Temp:** -19C (inside tent with heater). **Hours of light:** 20hr 04 min

For the first time since I fell through the ice, I feel vaguely warm, and the cold that had penetrated to my bones has lifted.

Strong winds and currents have pushed us 21 miles south in 24 hours, putting us two days behind schedule.

The *Daily Telegraph*
Monday, April 6, 1998

QUESTION 1
(20 marks for Reading)

Read David Hempleman-Adams' 'North Pole Diary' which was published in the *Daily Telegraph*. How successfully do you think the article informs and entertains the reader?

You should comment on:
▶ the language used, including any headlines
▶ the content and organization
▶ the overall design and layout
▶ any other aspects of the article which you think are relevant.

Main assessment objective

You need to show that you can:
▶ evaluate how information is presented.

Supporting assessment objectives

You also need to show that you can:
▶ read closely and carefully, referring to relevant details in texts
▶ respond to texts in a thoughtful and informed way
▶ follow an argument
▶ read between the lines to pick up what is hinted at as well as what is stated directly
▶ understand, describe and evaluate the various ways in which writers use language, structure and presentation to achieve particular effects.

QUESTION 2
(20 marks for Writing)

Range of writing: analyse, review, comment

What do you think are the reasons why some people take part in such dangerous activities as polar exploration, mountaineering, caving, and hang-gliding? Would you like to try such sports? Give reasons for your answer.

Main assessment objective

You need to show that you can:
▶ use a particular form of writing (a letter, a report, etc.) for a specific purpose.

Supporting assessment objectives

You also need to show that you can:
▶ communicate clearly
▶ organize your ideas into sentences and paragraphs
▶ use the grammatical structures of Standard English and a wide vocabulary to express what you want to say clearly and precisely.

QUESTION 3
(20 marks for Writing)

Range of writing: argue, persuade, instruct

You are a member of a team of students from your school which is organizing a four-week expedition to a remote part of the world. Because the cost of the expedition is high, it is necessary for the school to seek sponsorship from local businesses. Write a letter to **one** company asking for its support.

Your letter should persuade the company that the expedition is worthwhile in its own right and that the company itself will benefit from being associated with your expedition.

(You are free to make up any necessary details, such as your destination and the purpose of the expedition.)

Main assessment objective

You need to show that you can:
▶ adapt your writing for a particular purpose and audience.

Supporting assessment objectives

You also need to show that you can:
▶ communicate clearly
▶ organize your ideas into sentences and paragraphs
▶ use the grammatical structures of Standard English and a wide vocabulary to express what you want to say clearly and precisely.

Acknowledgements

The publishers would like to thank the following for permission to reproduce photographs:

Corbis UK Ltd/Jonathan Blair: pp 27 (left), 28 (left); **Corbis UK Ltd/Christiana Carvalho/FLPA**: p 119 (right); **Corbis UK Ltd/Stephanie Colesanti**: p 70 (right); **Corel Professional Photos**: pp 34, 70 (left); **Paul Grover**: p 119 (left); **Stephen Hawkins**: p 70 (middle); **The Kobal Collection/Universal**: p 104; **Northants Press Agency/Damien McFadden**: p 24; **Pictorial Press Ltd**: p 99 (both); **"PA" News/John Stillwell**: p 25; **Rex Features Ltd/Eric Pendzich**: pp 35, 36.

The authors and publisher are grateful to the following for permission to reprint copyright material:

Arcadia Group plc, for advert for Hawkshead Kids Boots; **Associated Press Ltd**, for photograph by Max Nash used on front page of *Daily Telegraph*, 25 June 1998; **Avon Cosmetics Ltd** for advertising slogan; **Beiersdorf UK Ltd**, for text from Nivea advertisement; **British Anti-Vivisection Association**, for advertisement 'Most people see a healthy human baby…'; **Brother UK**, for advertisement for the Fax-930; **Daihatsu (UK) Ltd**, for advert for the Daihatsu Terios; **Daily Mail/Solo Syndication Ltd** for article by Jenny Hope: 'The Passive Killer' and graphic from *Daily Mail*, 12 March 1998; headline and extract from 'Bangers and Rockets are Banned in New Bonfire Safety Drive' from *Daily Mail*, 15 October 1998; and various headlines from *Daily Mail* 25 November 1997, 25 September 1998, and 15 October 1998; **Encyclopedia Britannica International Ltd** for advertisement, produced for client Encyclopaedia Britannica International Ltd by agency DMS, Cheltenham, UK; **The Express**, for Leader masterhead and various headlines from *The Express*, 21 July 1998; **Futuroscope – The European park of the Moving Image**, for advertisement: 'Futuroscope – Destination sensation'; **The Guardian**, for headlines from *The Guardian*, 25 September 1998 and *The Guardian*, 15 October 1998, all copyright © *The Guardian* 1998; **Halfords Ltd**, for advertisement, 'To appreciate Halford's adjustable brake levers…'; **David Hempleman-Adams**, for article 'As I Fell into the Icy Sea My Nightmare Became Reality' from *The Daily Telegraph*, 6 April 1998; **Imation**, for advertisement for SuperDisk; **States of Guernsey Tourist Board**, for advertisement 'A breath of fresh air'; **La Redoute (UK) Ltd**, for advertisement for La Redoute – The French Fashion Collection: 'Don't run with the pack…'; **Lee Valley Regional Park Authority** for 1998 corporate advertising campaign; **Legoland Windsor**, for advertisement; **Leonard Cheshire Foundation**, for advertisement 'Enabled', © Leonard Cheshire Foundation, all rights reserved; **The London Dungeon**, for 'Ride the Nightmare' leaflet; **Matki** for 'Heavenly Showers' advertisement, reproduced by permission of Matki plc – Bristol; **Ministry of Transport**, for roadworks warning sign as used on front page of *Daily Telegraph*; **The Mirror**, for article by Tracey Harrison and Jeremy Armstrong: 'Stop Messing with our Natural Food', from *The Mirror*, 11 August 1998, and various headlines from *The Mirror*, 23 July 1998 and *The Mirror*, 15 October 1998; **Motts Travel of Aylesbury** and **Crusader Holidays of Clacton** for extract from 'Super Citybreaks' leaflet; **National Westminster Bank**, for bi-plane wing-walker advertisement; **Oxford Mail**, for articles by Matt Childe: 'Sorry Seems to be the Hardest Word: Elton Fans Furious at No Apology for Cancelled Concert' from *Oxford Mail*, 9 June 1998; and by Catherine McAlister: 'Why Men and Women Should Stop Trying to be More Like Each Other and Enjoy Being… Worlds Apart' from *Oxford Mail*, 1 July 1998; **Oxfordshire County Council**, for leaflet 'Have you ever felt sleepy while driving?', produced by Local Authorities in the South East of England; **Oxfordshire Nature Conservation Forum**, for cover of 'Action for Wildlife' leaflet, designed by Peter Creed of the Nature Conservation Bureau (Newbury); **Proctor and Gamble**, for adverts for Cover Girl Simply Powder Foundation and Marathon Lipcolor; **Radisson Edwardian**, for advertisement as used on front page of *Daily Telegraph*; **Royal National Institute for Deaf People**, for leaflet 'It's time to test your hearing'; **SAGA Insurance Services**, for leaflet advertising Saga Private Healthcare Plan; **Sandals**, for advertisement for Sandals Negril: 'Seven Miles of Serenity'; **Seebirds**, for advert for guided birdwatching holidays in Scotland; **Simply Computers Ltd**, for extract from leaflet; **The Telegraph Group / Ewan McNaughton Associates**, for article by Boris Johnson: 'It's all Dastardly Nonsense' from *Daily Telegraph*, 6 November 1997, and facsimile of front page of *Daily Telegraph*, 25 June 1998, all items © Telegraph Group Ltd, London 1997, 1998 except items 4, 10, 13 and article by S Steiner; **Telegraph Offers/Selective** for advertisement 'Christmas trees delivered direct to your door…'; **Times Newspapers**, for extracts from articles by Paul Stokes: 'Brother and Sister are Reunited after 50-year Separation', from *The Times*, 20 May 1998; by Michael Horsnell: 'Irate Fishermen Sink Sailor's Small Dream' from *The Times*, 20 May 1998; and by Paul Wilkinson: 'Tom Loses to Jerry as Mouse Bites Cat', from *The Times*, 30 July 1998; all © Times Newspapers Limited, 1998; **Travelsphere Ltd**, for advertisement 'A great deal to look at … for a great deal less!' © Travelsphere Ltd; **Value Retail Management (Bicester Village) Ltd**, for leaflet: 'Bicester Village international outlet shopping'; **World Vision**, for advertisements, '24 Hour Famine' and 'Alem's Life Chances'; **Yellow M**, for advertisement for Scarpa: 'Watch in comfort…'

Despite efforts to trace and contact copyright holders before publication this has not been possible in every case. If notified, the publisher undertakes to rectify any errors or omissions at the earliest opportunity.